BASIC ATTENDING SKILLS

(FOURTH EDITION)

Allen E. Ivey

Norma Gluckstern Packard

Mary Bradford Ivey

MICROTRAINING ASSOCIATES

Dedication

To: Bill and John Ivey

Amie Yabroff

Elizabeth Robey and Kathryn Quirk

Each of you has contributed in a special way to the development of microcounseling. Your participation, encouragement, and challenges have been part of Microtraining's growth.

Permission to paraphrase certain portions of this book have been granted by Charles C. Thomas Publishers, Springfield, Illinois. Videotapes to accompany this book are available from Microtraining Associates, Inc.

CONTENTS

Chapter 1   Basic Attending Skills: An Overview.   3

Chapter 2   Attending Behavior: The Foundation of Effective Listening   17

Chapter 3   Open Invitation to Talk   37

Chapter 4   Clarifying: The Minimal Encourage and Paraphrase   55

Chapter 5   Responding to Feelings and Emotions.   71

Chapter 6   Summarization: Integrating Client Behavior, Thoughts,
             and Feelings.   93

Chapter 7   Integration of Skills: Structuring an Effective Interview   109

Chapter 8   Teaching Helping Skills to Others.   131

Basic Attending Skills in Brief Summary Statements

#1 Attending Behavior   19

#2 Open Invitation to Talk.   39

#3 The Minimal Encourage   56

#4 The Paraphrase.   58

#5 Reflection of Feeling   74

#6 Summarization   94

#7 The Basic Listening Sequence   111

#8 The Five-Stage Interview Structure   112

Your first task in a helping relationship is to listen.

The second is to listen with individual and multicultural sensitivity.

Often your helpees will find their own way to resolve their issues because you listened.

CHAPTER 1

BASIC ATTENDING SKILLS: AN OVERVIEW

Basic Attending Skills is designed to provide you with a fundamental understanding and competence in the most important skills of helping, counseling, and therapy. Attending and listening skills provide a means for you to make contact with your clients and to hear them accurately. These skills are basic to *empathy,* the ability to be sensitive to and understand the world of another human being.

Many of us are tempted to provide immediate advice and suggestions to those who come to us with a troubling concern. We give them useful suggestions, only often to find ourselves disappointed and surprised when our good ideas are ignored. This book is not necessarily opposed to advice, but many people can solve their own problems if we simply listen to them carefully. Advice may not be needed!

Moreover, it is important to remember that client issues often developed over a period of time and may be more complex than we originally thought. Doesn't it make good sense just to stop for a while and hear clients out fully before we move to suggesting what can be done?

Let's test out the importance of listening in terms of your own life experience. Please think back on a time when someone listened to you and was truly helpful. If you can, seek to obtain an image of the helping situation and recall what you saw, heard, and felt. And, thinking back to that helpful time, reflect on what that person did to be helpful. This may help you connect personally with the value and power of really listening. Use the following lines for your recollections.

How does it feel to have someone truly listen to you? _____

_____

What specifically did the listener *do* that helped? _____

_____

The central maxim of this book and the helping process could be summarized as:

*Listen, listen, listen, and then listen some more
before taking action or giving advice.*

If you listen to and attend to others, many times they can resolve issues on their own. This book and training program is concerned with the growth potential that is in every helpee, client, or person. Listening to them and enabling them to find their strengths is basic to the helping process.

WHAT ARE THE BASIC ATTENDING SKILLS?

There are six major skill areas of listening in this book. A brief definition of each and its major function in the interview follows:

Definition and Function in the Interview

Attending Behavior

Individually and culturally appropriate verbal and nonverbal behavior in the interview is central to the helping process— eye contact, vocal tone, body language, and verbal following. This demonstrates that you are listening and encourages the client to talk more freely.

Open Invitation to Talk

Open questions often begin with *what, how,* or *could.* They help the client explore issues and talk at greater length. Closed questions often begin with *do, is, are* and lead to focused answers, often shorter in length.

Clarifying
—Encourage
—Paraphrase

Encourages are brief responses such as head nods, "uh-huh," and single words or phrases. They encourage client depth exploration and bring clarity as to meaning. The paraphrase feeds back to the client the essence of what has been said. The paraphrase provides a check on the accuracy of your listening and may enable the client to move on to a new topic.

Responding to Feelings and Emotion

Reflection of feeling is concerned with identifying and feeding back to the helpee the underlying emotional experience. Exploration of emotion is basic to understanding client deeper desires and wishes. Clarifying emotion leads to better client decision-making and action.

Summarization	This skill asks you to feed back to the client the essence of longer statements or a whole interview. Many summarizations will include descriptions of behavior, thoughts, and emotion. The skill is useful in clarifying what has happened in key interview segments and in beginning and ending the interview.
Integration of Skills —Five Stages of the Interview	The final segment of this program brings together the several skills above into a well-formed interview. You will find that it is possible to conduct a full interview using only listening skills.

These several skills add up to what is termed the *basic listening sequence.* Observation and research have revealed that not only effective counselors use these skills. The competent physician must listen to the patient before providing a diagnosis. The manager must listen to staff and learn important facts before making a critical decision.

The basic listening sequence taught in this book is critical in many different situations. If you listen carefully, you will often find that clients can resolve their own issues without advice or direction from you. If your clients don't come up with their own answers, you at least have an information base so that you can act more effectively.

Once you have studied and mastered each one of the basic listening skills above, this book provides advanced suggestions that can enable you to adapt the skills in a variety of situations. Special attention will be paid to the importance of drawing out client behaviors, thoughts, and feelings and, in practice sessions, applying these same skills to family therapy and to group work.

As you gain experience in the interview, you will find that a positive style of interviewing and listening tends to be more effective than just focusing of helpee problems and difficulties. Regardless of your work setting, you will find that if you focus on the positive, you provide your clients with a solid base on which they can then work more effectively with their most challenging issues.

THE POSITIVE ASSET SEARCH: POSITIVE PSYCHOLOGY IN ACTION

Beginning helpers occasionally have the tendency to become overly fascinated with "war stories," the basic facts about someone else's problems and concerns. It then follows that their questions, comments, and attention are given primarily to negative things about the helpee. It is fascinating to learn the intimate facts of someone else's life. But helping is not about prying into other people's affairs.

If you focus on "war stories," the helpee frequently jumps into your trap with glee, delighted that someone is finally listening to their problems. The naive helper's need to pry into another person's life *and* the helpee's need to share how "bad" the world is may result in a spiral that defines the situation as worse than it really is.

At the other extreme, some beginning helpers are so anxious to reassure helpees that real issues are never encountered. The rescuer is perhaps even more dangerous than the prying, probing helper. Many professional and volunteer helpers are so anxious to aid clients facing difficult issues that they gloss over and hide issues so the helpee "doesn't feel bad." Watch out for rescuing!

People talk about what other people will listen to. If a beginning counselor/helper only listens to weaknesses and problems, the client/helpee will only talk about weaknesses and problems. While airing of concerns is helpful and often necessary, it is only part of anyone's life picture. On the other hand, if the helper avoids hard issues, so does the helpee.

Positive psychology has become increasingly important as a central dimension of the field. If you seek out client strengths and help them build on these, you are taking positive psychology into action.

Another basic maxim of the helping process:

> *Helpees will talk about topics to which you are able and willing to listen.*
> *Watch out for prying and don't be a rescuer.*
> *Discover the positive assets of each client.*

Thus we believe a significant part of any helping interview should focus on strengths of the helpee to cope successfully with the world. This is true of even the most experienced professional. This means listening for positive as well as negative comments. For example:

Helpee: I really feel mixed-up and confused, nothing is going right. Society is all screwed up, the rich get richer and the poor get poorer. I worked hard, but I still get laid off.

Helper: (accentuating the negative) Society is really grim, you feel really hopeless. What are some of other things that bother you?

Helper: (accentuating the positive) Losing your job at a time like this is really hard. I hear you say you did good work. Could you share some specific things that you did on your past job which you were particularly proud of that can serve as strengths for the future?

Helper: (overly positive) Not to worry—it's always darkest before the dawn. (Rescuing) Let me do the worrying for a while. We'll find a way. What do you want me to do for you first?

The first response does acknowledge the feelings of desperation and hopelessness of the helpee and may well be a satisfactory response in a larger context. However, there are "would-be" helpers who only reinforce negative self-comments and troubles. The second response acknowledges the feelings, but also emphasizes the positive aspects of the situation, aiding the helpee in sorting out positive resources. The third response (reassurance) is often helpful, but can be overdone. This response fails to acknowledge the helpee's hurt and the helper has taken on too much responsibility for solving the client's difficulties.

A behaviorist summarized the issue when stating that love could be defined as giving positive reinforcement to positive things about an individual. The humanist also believes in human strength and seeks to encourage self-growth from those positive assets. Different words and theories . . . but the same idea. In any session, give some attention to what's right with the individual.

Another critical maxim for you to consider is:

> *Focus on the positive—search for strengths in the client*
> *and external supports in family and friends.*
> *Use those strengths and supports—*
> *They are the building blocks for the client's future.*

THE BASICS OF A PHILOSOPHY OF HELPING

The program you are entering is highly skill oriented. We have noted that some beginning helpers get worried about what they "should" be doing when relating to a client. They get so worried about doing the "right" thing that in the process they become confused and less effective. A basic philosophy of helping can be helpful. Some key suggestions leading toward this philosophy follow.

Honor yourself!

The first step toward effective helping is respecting yourself and your capacities. If you don't feel good about yourself, you are very unlikely to help those who come to you. You also need to focus on your strengths and build an interviewing helping style that fits you. Unless you are comfortable with yourself, you won't be able to help others. Many beginning and experienced helpers, counselors, and therapists find that they can benefit from counseling or therapy.

Each of us ultimately must define our own style of helping. When a skill or concept from this book appeals to you, go ahead and try it . . . but always be sure that it feels right to you. On the other hand, if that skill or concept doesn't appeal to you, it is still probably a good idea to try it and check it out thoroughly. But if you find it doesn't "fit," it is best to acknowledge that fact and stay with a style that is more natural to you.

Another important maxim:

> As a helper, you can be mostly helpful if you are truly yourself. Seek to define your own style of interviewing, but always with awareness that varying clients may respond to different styles than those with which you are most comfortable.

Honor the client

Most confusion around interviewing disappears if we are willing to listen carefully and attend to the client. When you find yourself confused, lost, or wondering what to do in the interview—listen and use the attending skills of this book.

The major temptation in helping is to attempt to solve the problem of the helpee as soon as possible. The beginning helper often barely gives the helpee time to get the problem out before starting to offer sympathy and solutions.

We urge you to stay away from giving early answers to those whom you would help. The use of advice, interpretation, or suggestions is for a later, more advanced, state of helping—and even then these skills should be used sparingly. *Our job is to listen.* Very few people in our society are effective listeners; it seems sad that we must teach people to listen, but it is a necessary skill that our culture does not emphasize.

Experienced professional counselors and therapists all-too-often are ineffective listeners. They may have become so fond of a special theory or method that they apply it to all clients, failing to see that what works with one person may not be effective with the next. And, we have seen many professionals who still have failed to master the basics of listening.

Finally, honoring your client may mean that you have to be uncomfortable sometimes as you adapt your personal interviewing style to the needs of the person before you. And, if you are not sufficiently comfortable with that client (or the client is not comfortable with you), it is important to refer the client carefully to someone else.

Another maxim:

> *Honoring and respecting your client may mean temporarily giving up your natural style and joining the client's world.*

Honor Multicultural Difference

Empathy asks you to listen carefully and join the client's world. We often talk about seeing the world as various helpees see it, hearing what they hear, and feeling what they feel. An important part of any person's personal identity is her or his multicultural heritage. We define multiculture broadly so as to consist of at least the following dimensions:

Race/ethnicity	Socioeconomic status
Gender	Age
Sexual identity	Family history
Physical ability/disability	Language
Religious/spiritual orientation	Traumatic life experiences

Each of these groups (and others) may approach the interview in a different way and may challenge your ability to be empathic and understand them. This is so, particularly, if you "haven't been there." For example, anyone who has experienced the traumatic life events of cancer, rape, or war belongs to a unique cultural group. Those who are raised in an alcoholic family have their own experiences. Your ability to win trust with people whose life experience, skin color, or sexual orientation is different from you may be challenging at times.

How can you build trust with someone who is substantially different from you? Consider the following as a beginning toward a lifetime of learning:

Listen. Ultimately, your ability to hear client stories and understand their world will be basic, regardless of multicultural background.

Be willing to share yourself openly. At times you need more than listening to build a trusting relationship. Many have found that direct and open acknowledgement of cultural difference can facilitate trust.

Avoid stereotyping. You will find that there is extensive variation in any multicultural group. Individual White Americans and Canadians are not the same, just as all Asian Americans or Asian-Canadians differ from each other. The interview and counseling are for the individual client, not for an imagined group.

Read, learn, participate. Multicultural understanding can only really develop if you commit yourself to studying and participating in the life of different cultural groups. This could include attending multicultural community events, a visit to a conservative or liberal church, or visiting an open Alcoholics Anonymous meeting.

How Will You Learn Basic Attending Skills?

In one sense, the concepts in this book are simple. The listening skills presented here are seen by most readers as crystal clear. Clarity does not mean that practice in these skills is not necessary. Just because you can understand the basics of attending does not mean you can use them when faced with a difficult and challenging client.

A crucial question to ask yourself is whether or not you are willing to do the work to become the most effective listener possible. Practice is essential for mastery. Providing "answers" and sympathy is easy; effective listening demands more effort.

The listening skills presented here are founded on nearly forty years of counseling and interviewing practice and over 450 research studies. The skills approach is termed "microcounseling" and breaks down the complex interview into component parts and teaches them one-at-a-time. The advantage of this process is that you can readily master specific concepts and methods that will make a difference in the lives of those with whom you work.

The microcounseling training system, as you will encounter it here, consists of the following steps:

1. *Introduction/Warm-up.* You will receive a brief introduction to a basic skill of interviewing. Learning objectives will be established.

2. *Reading about the skill.* A brief summary describes the key components of the interviewing skill you are about to learn.

3. *Viewing a model of the skill in action.* Seeing a person perform a helping skill can bring reading and theory into real life. Videotape models provide one way to see a skill in action. Live demonstrations by experts is another way. *Seeing is believing.*

4. *Practice.* Perhaps even more important than watching others is you taking time to practice the skills in each session. Specific suggestions and feedback sheets are provided to facilitate your learning the skills at a full mastery level. With some more complex skills, several practice sessions may be needed.

5. *Generalization.* Specific suggestions for taking the concepts of the training session to your home setting are included with each skill.

The first three steps focus on you learning the skill and should lead you to an understanding of why the skill is important and what it can do for you and your client. The last two steps, however, are the critical ones. There are many people who can develop an intellectual understanding of the helping process—but understanding is not competence in the interview.

The competent, effective interviewer practices the skills to a level of mastery and is able to take the ideas of the skill "home" to his or her daily life and work setting.

ETHICAL ISSUES AS YOU PRACTICE SKILLS

Practice is central to mastery of the skills in this book, but when you practice you are working with real people. This is not a book on ethics, but we'd like to introduce some key issues. For further study of ethical issues, we recommend *Issues & Ethics in the Helping Professions* by G. Corey, M. Corey, & P. Callanan (Pacific Grove, CA: Brooks/Cole 2003).

Some key issues to consider include:

Competence.   You are a beginning interviewer. In these early stages do not attempt to do therapy and seek to keep your practice interviews to topics around which both you and the volunteer client are comfortable. Be ready to refer your volunteer to a more experienced helper. Always seek supervision and consultation on these issues with your teacher or workshop leader.

Recording and Informed consent.   When you work with a volunteer practice client, it is very helpful if you can record the session. Volunteers need to know that this is a *practice interview*. Obtain permission before you record a session or write a transcript of what has been recorded. If you are relaxed about this request, they will be as well. Clients should be informed that you will turn off recording equipment at any point if they are uncomfortable. You may even wish to develop a written consent form, as this practice is becoming more common in counseling and therapy in general.

Confidentiality.   As this is practice, you obviously do not have legal confidentiality. But, even so, it is vital that you keep the information learned in the interview to yourself and only share it with classmates or teachers if you have the consent of the volunteer. If the volunteer should indicate that he or she may do harm to self or others or otherwise engage in illegal acts, it is your duty to break confidentiality and seek consultation with your supervisor.

MICROCOUNSELING: A BRIEF SUMMARY
OF KEY THEORETICAL CONCEPTS

We are often asked if microcounseling is a theory and mode of helping in itself or if it is merely a set of practical skills. We believe that the concepts presented here are both theoretically significant and practical. Microcounseling was first developed as a set of skills, which could be used in conjunction with other theories. This belief is still primary—regardless of the theory you select, you will find that the listening skills here are invaluable in being an effective helper, counselor, or therapist.

However, microcounseling can be viewed as a theory and method of helping in itself. Defining theory can be said to rest on three key questions?

1. Does the system organize knowledge about helping in a fashion so that it can be used in many different settings and situations?

The microskills presented here are used in many settings ranging from counseling and therapy to medical training to business management education. All these fields need effective listening. The concepts have been translated into at least seventeen languages and have been used effectively in Japan, Germany, and North America with a range wide of populations. The microskills system has proven effective in workshops with multicultural groups of many types in the United States and Canada, through managers in Sweden, teachers and nurses in Japan, Inuit and Dene social workers in the Central Arctic, and AIDS and refugee counseling in Africa.

2. Does the system contain a basic set of assumptions that can analyze, predict, or explain what happens in the helping process?

You will find, if you use certain helping skills in the interview, that you can predict what clients may be expected to say in return. You will also find that following the recommended five-stage interviewing sequence will often result in clients generating new perceptions of themselves and others.

3. Does the system explain what happens in the practice of interviewing, counseling, and therapy?

Microcounseling theoretical goals have traditionally been modest. Nonetheless, the framework explains some of the basics of effective helping. Whether you practice listening as a counselor, social worker, pastoral counselor, financial adviser, or as a child advocate in court, the listening skills presented here remain central.

Put most concisely, helpees often come to us with tight and narrow ways of thinking about their problems. If we listen to them effectively, they will likely loosen the old and ineffective ways of thinking—they will generate new ways of perceiving themselves, their situations, and others.

The acts of attending and listening are very powerful. Through your careful listening, the client will come to find new perspectives and ways of being in the world. The generation of new perspectives and ways of thinking is at the heart of *Basic Attending Skills*. This is a simple, but profound, part of any comprehensive theory of helping.

SUGGESTED REFERENCES

Ivey, A., Gluckstern, N., and Ivey, M. (1997). *Basic Influencing Skills.* North Amherst, Massachusetts: Microtraining.

This book, and accompanying videotape series, has been designed as a follow-up program to *Basic Attending Skills.* Skills such as interpretation, self-disclosure, and assertiveness training will be found plus brief workshop sessions around empathic dimensions such as concreteness, immediacy, and confrontation.

Ivey. A., & Ivey, M. (2003). *Intentional Interviewing and Counseling.* (5th Edition) Pacific Grove, Ca.: Brooks/Cole.

The logical follow-up from *Basic Attending Skills* and *Basic Influencing Skills,* this more advanced book covers the listening and influencing skills in full detail. An interactive CD-ROM is available.

Evans, D. Hearn, M., Uhlemann, M., and Ivey, A. (2004). *Essential Interviewing: A Programmed Approach to Effective Communication.* (6th Edition) Pacific Grove, Ca.: Brooks/Cole.

A programmed text elaborating on microskill concepts—highly useful for practicing listening and influencing skills.

Ivey, A. (1995). *Managing Face to Face Communication: Survival Tactics for People and Products in the 21st Century.*

Application of attending and influencing skills in business. Videotapes for management education available.

Ivey, A., D'Andrea, M., Ivey, M., and Simek-Downing, L. (2002). *Theories of Counseling and Psychotherapy: A Multicultural Perspective.* Englewood Cliffs, N.J.: Prentice-Hall.

Introductory text based on the microskills model that includes information on how the skills are sequenced and used in varying psychological theories. This text is known for its specifics on multicultural issues.

*Attending behavior is the
foundation of listening.*

*But attending behavior needs
to be varied to meet
individual and cultural styles.*

CHAPTER 2

ATTENDING BEHAVIOR: THE FOUNDATION OF EFFECTIVE LISTENING

The first thing that the helper must learn is to *listen* to the helpee. But what is listening? We all know what it is when it happens, but defining the term precisely is another matter. The central goal of this first session in microtraining is to help you identify specifically what listening is and to consider the many implications of this definition.

The exercises and readings in this chapter will help you to:

1. Understand the importance of effective listening.

2. Define four central dimensions of attending behavior and identify some critical individual and cultural differences underlying effective attending.

3. Understand the critical concept of selective attention. Clients will tend to talk about topics to which you are willing to listen.

4. Demonstrate attending behavior yourself in a practice individual interview. You are also encouraged to practice these concepts in a group session.

5. Use attending behavior in your daily life and also to consider how you might teach the skill to others.

WHAT LISTENING IS *NOT!*

One effective way to discover the nature of listening is through examining what it is *not*. Find another person and go through the following exercise or watch the behavior of another pair:

Person 1: Interviewer/helper   However, the task is to do the *worst* job of listening possible. It helps to exaggerate. You may also want to think of an individual who talked to you in real life and did a very poor job of hearing what you had to say.

Person 2: The client/helpee	Regardless of how poorly the interviewer behaves, your task is to keep talking.
Suggested topics for the brief two-minute role-play	A job interview, a discussion of a family conflict, choice of courses, or a topic of mutual interest to the helper and the helpee.

List below your observations of what helping/counseling isn't. After you make your list, check to see if what your list represents is observable behavior, something that you can see (e.g., the helper may appear anxious—true, but what do you *see* that makes you think he/she is anxious? Wringing the hands, sitting tensely, stammering?).

Specific observable behaviors that represent ineffective listening:

_____

_____

_____

_____

After discussions with others and obtaining reactions from the helpee, you may want to add to the above list. As a final step, look over the list and note the things that you think most important. Underline those you would stress if you were teaching basic helping skills. In the following reading, you'll see what research and practice have found to be most basic. However, it is also important to remember your own list for it is uniquely yours and provides some important clues as to your own approach to analyzing and teaching the interview.

The following *Basic Skill* description lays a foundation for becoming a helper. The behaviors described are bedrocks for effective listening. Without the following skills, even the most brilliant helper may fail.

ATTENDING BEHAVIOR: BASIC SKILL #1

The most basic skill of helping is listening to those whom you attempt to help. But what is listening? We use the term "attending behavior" to remind us that listening consists of specific and observable dimensions. Attending behavior is a basic, rather simple skill—but with many, many profound implications.

Four key dimensions comprise attending behavior:

1. *Eye contact.* If you are going to talk to someone, look at him or her. No need to stare, just be aware that you are talking to another person. You'll also want to notice *eye contact breaks.* When you look away you are sometimes telling the person you are working with that you aren't really attending (but don't stare—some natural breaks do occur). Later on, you'll start noticing that eye contact breaks on the part of helpees give you clues as to where that person "is at." More on that later.

2. *Attentive body language.* We usually think that counseling is a verbal relationship. In truth, some estimates say that 85% of our communication is nonverbal. Think for a minute—how does your body communicate that it is listening? Find your own natural listening style and check with others to see how it "comes across." The basic attentive listening posture in our culture is a slight forward trunk lean with a relaxed easy posture. But find your own style—if you are not true to yourself, you won't appear attentive to your client.

    Later on you'll want to start looking for small signs of tension (frowns, tense mouth or chin, clenched fists, marked shifts in body posture at key times in the interview) in both yourself and the client. But for now, simply assume a relaxed body position and communicate that you are involved. Your awareness of body language will naturally increase throughout this training series.

3. *Vocal style.* Changes in speech rate, volume, and tone often indicate interest or disinterest. Speech hesitations or stammers often occur at tension points. The music of emotion and feeling is often most apparent through the voice.

4. *Verbal following.* A frequent basic question of beginning helpers is "What do I say?" We say, *relax*—it doesn't help to be nervous. When in doubt as to what to say, take whatever the helpee has said and respond to it in a natural way. Direct whatever you may say to what the helpee has just said or perhaps said earlier in your session. *The helper seldom needs to introduce a new topic.*

    Your prime task is simply to stay with what has already been said. In summary, don't topic jump!

Cultural differences. It is critical that you remember that the attending behavior of different cultural and ethnic groups varies in style. Eye contact among some Southwest Native Americans may represent a hostile act, the physical distance between two speakers may vary from culture to culture (e.g., people from the Middle East stand much more closely together than middle-class people in the U.S.) and the standard vocal tone of American English may be slow and boring to some Latina/o peoples. Attending behavior appears to be a universal cultural phenomenon. However, attending skills manifest themselves differently among different people.

The following chart summarizes only some key differences in listening skills among different groups. And, as you read the following, recall that individual differences within a group vary extensively. Avoid stereotyping your client.

Eye Contact	Traditional African-Americans, Latina/o, and Native Americans may avoid eye contact as a sign of respect. With Latina/o's, direct sustained eye contact can represent a challenge to authority. A bowed head may be a sign of respect from Native Americans.
Body Language	African-Americans may have public behavior that seems emotionally intense and demonstrative to European-Americans. A slap on the back may be insulting to an Asian American or Latina/o.
Vocal Style	Latina/o's often begin meetings with lengthy greetings and pleasant talk before getting down to key issues. European-

| | Americans tend to value quiet, controlled vocal style that other groups may see as manipulative and/or cold. |
| Verbal following | Asian-Americans may prefer a more indirect and subtle communication and consider the African-American or European-American styles too direct and confrontive. Personal questions may be especially offensive to Native Americans. |

Individual differences. Similarly, individual helpees vary in their attending patterns. A depressed client will have difficulty in maintaining eye contact with you at all and likely have one topic—how bad things are. A client talking about an embarrassing or difficult issue may avoid eye contact and topic jump. When one combines individual and cultural variation, it is obvious that this most basic skill of listening can become very complex.

Thus it is suggested that not only do you demonstrate attending behavior yourself, but that you also *observe the attending patterns of others.* You may find that what seems to be rude or distant behavior is simply culturally appropriate patterns on the part of the other person and your own style may be interpreted by the client as even more rude. And, as your observation skills increase, you will note vast individual differences in patterns of attention on the part of your helpees, regardless of culture. Attending behavior provides a framework for observing your own behavior and the behavior of your clients.

Summary. In briefer form, your goal in interviewing is to be a good listener through the use of specific, observable behaviors that are culturally appropriate:

1. Use varied eye contact to communicate with the helpee. Be aware that different cultural groups may have varying patterns of eye contact.

2. Maintain an attentive body posture using a natural *relaxed* posture and gestures. Use your body to communicate your involvement.

3. Use a natural vocal style. Your voice communicates your emotions.

4. Stay on the topic. Don't topic jump or interrupt. Simply note what the helpee has said and take your cues from him/her. There is no need to go into your own head to think of what to say. The helpee has already told you.

If you get confused and can't think of anything to say, simply hesitate a moment and think back to something said earlier that interested you. Make a comment or ask a question about that topic. You are still attending! This simple point is a life-saver for both beginning helpers and highly experienced professionals.

WHERE DO YOU FOCUS YOUR ATTENTION?

The purpose here is to summarize some further implications of attending behavior with special reference to individual helper "style." The essential point of this manual is summarized below:

> *Helpees talk about what helpers listen to.* At first glance attending and attending skills impress the beginner as "non-directive" in nature. Attending skills lead as much as they follow.

For example, a client may say "I'm doing really poor work in school this past month. I'm really uptight right now. Things are going bad at home—Mom and Dad are talking divorce." Before going further, write below what you might say to this client.

I would say _____

_____

Compare your responses with the five following possibilities below which all attend to the client in some way:

1. "In what subjects are you having the most problems?"

2. "You're tense right now."

3. "Sounds like right now you're really concerned about what your parents fighting means for you?"

4. "What specifically is going on at home?"

5. "What type of work does your Dad do?"

The response selected by the helper often says more about the helper than it does about the helpee. Notice what topics you selectively attend to. What topics turn you on, turn you off? What do you zero in on? What do you avoid?

In the example above, the first response above focuses on schoolwork, the next two on the feelings of the client in the interview, the last two on the family context. All of the responses are attending and potentially helpful, but each response focuses on the problem from a different vantage point.

It is important to note the topics to which you attend and those that you tend to ignore. In the example above, schoolwork, the helpee's personal feelings, and the family context are all important. Nonetheless, most experts believe it is most important to focus on the feelings and thoughts of the client sitting there in front of you (#2 and #3 above). Was your first focus on the client, the school problem, the family, or some other issue?

The three aspects of attending behavior provide you with important cues as to what your "style" is. For example, where do you break eye contact? Do you unconsciously avert your eyes when someone talks about religion, thereby indicating this is a topic you don't care to hear about? Do your eyes brighten when the helpee talks about sex and you find that all your helpees are talking about this area? Careful examination of videotapes will reveal clear points where you reinforce certain helpee comments and extinguish others.

Similarly, note your pattern of body language in relation to specific topics. When do you sit forward, move back, tighten a fist, or relax? What does your body language communicate to your helpee? You'll find your body often mirrors that of your client if you are truly listening. This is termed "movement synchrony" and is a variable which can only really be studied by videotape.

The examples above illustrate the importance of selective attention in verbal following. *Once again, helpees talk about topics that you are willing and able to listen to.*

Constantly monitor your patterns of selective attention both verbally and nonverbally. It will give you a clue as to your natural "style." Finally, note your "percent of talk-time." Some helpers talk too much. Attending is about listening. Do you give your helpee enough "air-time" on topics of interest to her or him?

Audio or videorecord a practice session and note how much you talk and how much the client talks in a session. Use your watch or a stop watch and check it out.

USING ATTENDING BEHAVIOR SKILLS WITH FAMILIES AND GROUPS

Increasingly, helpers are being called on to work with groups and families. Attending behavior skills are just as important in these settings as with an individual. Most helpers learn individual interviewing first. Individual work focuses on the single helpee. Frequently beginning family and group workers focus solely on individuals and their problems, ignoring the potential power of the group.

As you work with the skills in this book, pause frequently to recall that the same skills are useful in family and group work. Following are some important issues in using attending beyond individual interviewing.

Do you balance your attending? Do you look at all group and family members or are there some few individuals who have the vast majority of your attention? Many helpers who move from individual work to family work falter when they give one or two people their primary attention. Some helpers give more attention to women in families, others to men. Some totally ignore children in family groups.

What are the attending behavior patterns in the group or family? You will find that certain members of the family or group are sought for leadership, particularly on certain topics. You will find that people who tend to have alliances in the family or group have similar patterns of body posture and may mirror one another. Those who are in conflict in the group will tend to avert eye contact and show signs of bodily tension.

Constantly practice your observations of nonverbal behavior. You will find that family and group members respond differently to you personally. These data can be a clue to your own effectiveness and may even give you information as to culturally appropriate behavior if the group or family comes from a different background than you. Also, be aware of your behavior—the group is!

Are there multicultural issues in the group? Again, recall that multicultural issues are critical in the helping process. You will want to learn specifics of the cultural group with which you are working. Not only is it possible that their patterns of eye contact and body language are different from your own, but who talks after whom can be important. In some cultures, the father is expected to speak for the family as a whole while with others the situation may be very different.

Working in a multicultural setting such as Canada or the U.S. provides helpers with the opportunity for a lifetime of learning about differences in attending styles. Group work with those from the Canadian Atlantic Provinces, California, and the Southern States varies. Men and women's groups have different styles, just as African-American, Latino, and White groups will vary.

Can you attend to the family or group as a whole? Essentially, learn to focus your attention on the entire "family" or "group." Deliberately use statements that contain the words "family" and "group"—"This group/family seems to feel anxious about meeting together." "The group/family seems to be good at supporting each other."

One general rule for family and group work is that one-third of the time should be spent on the total process of the group (with a focus on the words "family" and "group"); one-third of the time should be spent on individuals in the group and their behavior, thoughts, and feelings; and one-third of the time on the group's special topic or problem.

Thus, if you are working with a group of teens that come from alcoholic families, you will want to balance your attention to the three topics. Equal time and attention can be given to the general problem of alcoholism and the family, the individual problems of the teens, and to the group process itself.

CLASSIFYING ATTENDING AND NON-ATTENDING STATEMENTS

Imagine that you are working with a helpee who makes the following statements. Which of the following are attending and which are non-attending? (See page 34 for our answers.)

1. Helpee: I just had a terrible argument with my roommate. She's such a mess and leaves stuff all over the place. But, this last time, she went too far . . .

    _____ a. Helper: You say she went too far . . . what happened?

    _____ b. Helper: I think I can help you learn to get along.

2. Helpee: I'm not doing well in biology and I want to drop the course, but they say it's required for nursing. I'm really doing badly.

_____ a. Helper: Biology is required for nursing. Could you tell me a bit more about how much you want to be a nurse?

_____ b. Helper: I can help you change majors without much problem.

3. Helpee: My parents are giving me a bad time about my friends. They say that they are into drugs and they really aren't. We do have fun, but nothing serious.

_____ a. Helper: It sounds to me as if you may not be giving them or me a straight story.

_____ b. Helper: You are twenty-one. You can make your own decisions.

4. Helpee: My boss is difficult. He grabbed at me yesterday. I pushed him off, but I really need this job as it pays pretty well and keeps me in school. How can I handle this?

_____ a. Helper: Quit the job.

_____ b. Helper: Tell me a bit more about the situation. How are you handling things thus far?

5. Helpee: I'm feeling really sad lately. I can't sleep and even sometimes I cry for no reason at all. Things just aren't right.

_____ a. Helper: I hear you feel sad and that things aren't right for you. Tell me more.

_____ b. Helper: I'll refer you to a physician and see if some drugs can help.

PRACTICING ATTENDING BEHAVIOR

You have now seen negative examples of attending behavior and read about the possibilities inherent in the concepts. Hopefully, you will have had the opportunity to view a live demonstration, film, or videotape of the skill in action. But what is most important is your ability to engage in attending skills. The following is suggested to practice attending behavior.

1. *Develop a working group.* You can't practice attending behavior alone. The most effective group size is three or four. However, two people can be sufficient for practice.

2. *Assign roles for the first practice session.* The following are listed in order of critical importance:

    a. *Helper.* This individual practices attending behavior in a short role-play.

    b. *Helpee.* This person serves as client and discusses real or role-played concerns. The helpee also provides feedback to the helper after the role-play.

    c. *Observer/operator.* This person operates the videotape or audiotape equipment and provides verbal and written feedback to the helper. If no equipment is available, the emphasis is solely on observation.

    d. *Second observer.* This individual provides written feedback to the helper and ideally concentrates observations on nonverbal dimensions which may be missed by others. This is especially important if no videotape is available for practice.

3. *Determine topic for role-play.* The helpee decides what he or she would like to talk about in the brief role-play. While any topic may be suitable, we suggest that you use past and present vocational interests and jobs. The task of the helper is to enable the helpee to talk freely. As you gain more experience with the skills, select increasingly challenging topics. Attitudes to or experiences with alcohol and drugs is a very useful area that virtually all helpers will encounter.

4. *Watch time carefully and provide feedback.* The role-play should be approximately 3–4 minutes in length and video or audio-recorded. If not recorded, the observers become especially important to provide feedback. Use the feedback sheets provided and give specific information to the helpee. Do not be judgmental (e.g., "That was a great job!"). Rather, attempt to be specific and concrete (e.g., "You maintained eye contact and the client responded with a gradually relaxing body posture and vocal tone.").

5. *Rotate roles* so that every person has an opportunity to serve as helper and helpee. Again, remember to divide time for practice equally.

GROUP/FAMILY PRACTICE IN ATTENDING BEHAVIOR

Basic Attending Skills does not claim to make you an expert group or family inter-viewer or counselor. However, whether you are a beginner or even an advanced expert, some time spent deliberately working with the skills of this book can make you more effective with groups and families.

1. *Develop a working group.* For practice, a working group of four is recom-mended, a facilitator and three group members.

2. *If possible, assign two additional roles for the practice session.*

   a. *Observer/operator.* This person operates the videotape or audiotape equipment and provides verbal and written feedback to the group. If no equipment is available, the emphasis is solely on observation.

   b. *Second observer.* This individual provides written feedback to the helper and ideally concentrates observations on nonverbal dimen-sions that may be missed by others.

3. *Determine topic for role-play.* A useful and stimulating topic for the group can be taken from the alcohol and drug area—a working topic might be "the meaning of alcohol," but the specific topic should be decided on by the group and its leader.

4. *Planning.* Divide the time between the topic (alcohol suggested in this case), the individuals in the group (their feelings and attitudes toward alco-hol), and the group itself (how the group interacts as a whole). For this first practice exercise, follow time guidelines carefully. In the beginnings of fam-ily and group work, you will find that a firm structure is useful and helps make the group or family sense themselves as a "group" rather than just a collection of individuals.

5. *Watch time carefully and provide feedback.* The role-play group session should be approximately 30 minutes in length and video or audio-recorded. If not recorded, the observers become especially important to provide feedback. Complete the feedback sheets provided and give specific infor-mation to the helpee.

ATTENDING BEHAVIOR FEEDBACK SHEET

1. *Attending Behavior Counts*

As you view an interview live or on videotape, count the several attending behaviors. In this first exercise, look for problems in attending.

Attending Dimension	Number of Distracters in Ineffective Demonstration	Number of Distracters in Effective Demonstration	Additional Sessions			
Inappropriate eye contact breaks						
Distracting body movements						
Vocal style distractions						
Topic jumps						
Total non-attending behaviors						

2. *Percent of talk time.* Use a stopwatch to record talk-time. What percent of the conversation did the helper talk? _____

3. *Subjective Attending Observations*

   Patterns of eye contact. Appropriate, inappropriate, staring, avoiding? On what topics did the person break eye contact?

   _____

   _____

   _____

Physical attention. What do you see in terms of body movement, trunk lean, and hand or leg movements? Did you see any specific movements (e.g. physical withdrawal or moving forward) in relation to helpee's statements?

_____

_____

_____

Vocal tone/speech hesitations. General comments on vocal tone. Did you note any specific changes in vocal tone as the helper responded to the helpee? At what points did speech hesitations appear?

_____

_____

_____

Topic jumps/verbal following. Was the helper able to stay on the topic and not give advice or suggestions? How many topic jumps occurred? Who initiated topic jump changes?

_____

_____

_____

Selective Attention. Are there certain topics toward which the helper seems to demonstrate more extensive attending behavior? Are there places where the helper seems to lessen attending behavior and avoid a topic?

_____

_____

_____

4. *What were the strengths?* What did the helper do right? What do you notice as particular individual strengths in the interview?

_____

_____

_____

DO-USE-TEACH CONTRACT

DO: The First Dimension

You first had an opportunity to understand the concept of attending behavior through reading. You then experienced the ideas of attending behavior first hand through practice. This is the *do* portion of the Do-Use-Teach Contract. If you can *demonstrate* attending behavior in the practice session, you have achieved the first dimension of competence in attending.

USE: Taking the Concepts to the Real World

Now is the time to decide what these concepts mean to you and how they can be used in your own life space. We know from past experience and extensive research that the concepts are important and make a significant difference in the interview. But, can you take these ideas and use them beyond reading and the classroom or workshop session? What we'd like you to do now is think about how you might *use* the concepts of attending behavior outside the interview.

Ways that people have used attending behavior in their own lives include:

> A beginning helper tried attending in an interview when she didn't know what to do. She simply asked a question about something the client just said.

> A shy person who couldn't talk to anyone tried attending and found it provided an opening wedge in conversation.

> A man in trouble with his boss tried deliberate attending and discovered he was missing some crucial messages.

> At the family dinner table, a husband and wife found they weren't listening to their children and then used attending to open up the family interaction.

> A depressed individual found that going out and deliberately attending to someone else helped him get out of himself. (We have found that teaching attending skills is particularly useful in work with clients who show slight, moderate, or severe depression.)

> A student deliberately attended to her teacher and to her surprise found the teacher talking to her and no one else!

Personal experience with using attending is crucial. Our helping skills should not be used just in the interview; they have meaning in our daily lives as well.

What do you want to do to test out the value of attending in your own life? Write a specific plan and outline in detail how you will make the concepts relevant to you.

My plan to use attending behavior in my own life is _____

_____

_____

Talk with someone about your plan to use attending. Is it specific enough? Will it work? Can you arrange a time to get together with this individual to report how your contract worked out?

TEACH: Helping Others Grow

Next we would like you to think about someone or some group with whom you might like to test your understanding and facility with attending behavior by teaching them what you have learned in this chapter.

Teaching someone else about attending behavior has taken many forms:

Using this same workshop format to teach teachers, parents, peer facilitators, hot-line operators, etc., these listening skills that you have learned.

Labeling listening skills in your own way. After all, you don't have to use the terms eye contact, body language, and verbal following. Some might prefer very different use of words.

If you are helping someone in a counseling session, try teaching these basic skills. Teaching attending is especially helpful to depressed individuals or those with weak social and interpersonal skills. When clients attend to someone else, they are not attending to their own difficulties.

Teaching your clients listening skills can be very helpful. For some clients, learning how to listen may be more important than traditional counseling. To whom and when would you like to teach attending behavior? And how would you do it? Write a contract with someone in the group to actually set up a teaching plan.

My teaching plan is:

_____

_____

_____

DO—USE—TEACH

You don't know what you are doing until you can teach it to someone else.

Answers to Classification Items on Pages 25–26

1. A is attending
2. A is attending
3. A is attending
4. B is attending
5. A is attending

Note that in most of the examples above, the error of the helper who failed to attend was that her or his response tried to solve the problem much too early. In attending, we really want to draw out the helpee's issues in more detail before moving to problem solving.

*An open invitation to talk is
a gift to the client.*

*But, sometimes that gift
of questioning becomes "grilling"
and may be intrusive.*

*How are you going
to find a balance?*

CHAPTER 3

OPEN INVITATION TO TALK

Questions help an interview move along. They open new areas for discussion, they assist in pinpointing issues, and they can be used to facilitate helpee self-exploration. In recent years, questioning approaches to counseling and therapy have gained increased favor. Many cognitive counselors or family therapists, for example, may use as much as fifty percent questioning in their sessions. At the same time, it must be remembered that a few practitioners, primarily from a humanistic orientation, have suggested that the helper should *never* ask questions. One of your central tasks in this session will be to define where you stand on the use of questions.

The exercises and readings in this chapter will help you to:

1. Develop awareness of both strengths and weaknesses of questioning skills. You will be asked to generate your own position on the use of questions in the interview.

2. Define the difference between open and closed questions.

3. Identify how different questions stems ("Could," "What," "How," and "Why") tend to lead to varying types of client talk.

4. Demonstrate the skills of question asking in a practice interview. You are also encouraged to test these skills in practice with couples, groups, and family.

5. Use questioning skills in your daily life, and consider how you might teach the skills to others, including your clients.

What Are Your Feelings and Experiences With Questions?

In North American society, questions come endlessly. Children ask us questions almost as their first sentences, teachers question us in school, our employers question our performance and skills, and in the evening we watch television entertainers use questions to bring out their guests. Clearly, questions are an important part of our culture.

Questions also indicate that a person is interested in you and what you have to say. Good questions help people explore themselves and their feelings more deeply.

Yet, questions have varying impact on different people. Some feel put "on the spot" or "grilled" when someone asks them questions. If you have not established a solid base of trust with another person or a client, questions used too early can interfere with the development of rapport. If you are working with a client who is culturally different from you, it may be helpful to save questions until some trust is established.

Take some time to note both your positive and negative experiences with questions below. Has your personal experience with questions been mainly positive or negative?

My personal experience with questions has been:

Positives: _____

_____

_____

Negatives: _____

_____

_____

The position taken in this book is that questions are a helpful and necessary part of most interviews, but that we all must be aware of their limitations. Skilled question asking can result in clients learning how to question and examine themselves. Let us now consider more information about the critical skills of questioning.

OPEN INVITATION TO TALK: BASIC SKILL #2

The client comes into an interview with a concern or problem. The initial task of the interviewer is to stay out of the client's way so as to find out how the client sees the situation and defines the issues. Most useful in this process is the technique of providing limited structure through the use of an open invitation to talk.

Compare the following examples focused on interpersonal relationships:

> Open: Could you tell me about your relationship? How are you feeling toward her/him? What are some things you like about her/him?

> Closed: How long have you been together? Do you argue a lot? Does he/she understand you?

The open questions provide room for the client to express what is going on without the imposed categories of the helper. An open comment allows the client an opportunity to explore self and situation.

Closed questions, on the other hand, too often emphasize factual content as opposed to feelings. They may demonstrate a lack of interest in what the client has to say, and they frequently attack or put the client in his/her place. Closed questions can often be answered in a few words or with a yes or no. However, they can still be useful at times to fill in details.

Questions generally should be designed to help the client explore issues, rather than to merely provide information for the interviewer. If you rely on closed questions to structure the interview, you will find yourself forced to concentrate so hard on thinking up the next question that you may fail to hear what the client had to say.

Open invitations to talk are extremely useful in a number of different situations. The following are some examples:

1. They help begin an interview. (Could you tell me what you'd like to talk about today? How have things been since the last time we talked together?)

2. They help get the interviewee to elaborate on a point. (Could you tell me more about that? How did you feel when that happened?)

3. They help elicit examples of specific behavior so that the helper is better able to understand what the client is describing. (Will you give me a specific example? What do you do when you get "depressed?" How do you behave? What do you mean when you say your father is hard to get along with?)

4. They help focus the client's attention on feelings. (What are you feeling as you're telling me this? How did you feel then?)

5. Questions may help you find client thinking patterns that are not immediately obvious. (What were you thinking when you said that to your boss? What thoughts were in your mind while you did that? What were you saying to yourself when the boss spoke to you and you stayed silent?)

Go through the examples above again, and change them to closed questions. This exercise will help you note distinctions and differences between open and closed questions.

VARYING QUESTIONING CAN HELP CLIENTS EXPLORE ISSUES

During your next practice session, it will help if you explore various types of questions. Try asking a variety of open and closed questions. We would especially like you to try questions beginning with "how," "what," and "could" which most in the field believe give more room for helpee exploration than "why." For example, consider the different possibilities if you are asking a helpee about his or her job:

Could you tell me how things are going at work?

What are some of the things that trouble you about your job?

How do you feel about your boss?

Why do you think the boss treats you this way?

Or consider a marital counseling session:

"Could you share an example of a typical argument?"

"What did you do when he/she struck you?"

"How did you feel when he/she cried?"

"Why are you staying in the relationship?"

Could questions tend to be maximally open and pass on control to the client ("Could you tell me more?" "Could you give me an example?"). Research reveals that *could* questions put focus on the client in a comfortable way and seem to establish trust. Technically, could questions can be answered with a "yes" or "no," but relatively few clients stop there. *Could* questions seem to empower the client to answer questions as he or she wishes.

You may note that questions beginning with "could" might be interpreted as closed. A client may respond to this question with a simple "no" and say nothing more to this question. However, in North American culture, the "could" question tends to function most often as an open invitation to talk. "Could" questions have the special advantage of giving the control even more to the client as the word "could" implies that the client can decide whether or not to respond at all.

What questions often lead the helpee to talk about facts and specifics about a situation or event. Facts provide the foundation so that you know more precisely what occurred for your client. ("What happened?")

How questions most often lead to helpee talk about process and sequence or emotions ("How did that happen?" "How do you feel about that?"). Emotions are the motor of behavior and clients can get into their issues much more deeply when we help them explore their feelings.

Why questions typically ask clients to search for reasons underlying their behavior, thoughts, or emotions? Why questions and their search for reasons may put people on the spot. They are sometimes difficult to answer for we don't always know why others or we do things. What, how, and could questions provide more room, and providing space for growth is one basic dimension of being an effective helper.

You will find that clients hesitate longer if you ask them "why." Researchers suggest that "why" leads to an internal search. At the same time, you will find many effective helpers using why questions. Many clients gain benefit from understanding the reasons underlying their actions. Again you will have to make your own personal decisions whether or not you chose to use why questions.

A balance of open and closed questions is suggested in the early phases of an interview. Further, the open question "could" often provides the best overview of the situation. Later in the interview, you will often find helpees talking in relatively vague terms about a problem ("I don't get along with my lover/boss/ etc."). An open question seeking specifics ("Could you give me a specific example?") often proves to be extremely effective in defining the problem more clearly.

The multicultural dimension and establishing a relationship. As noted earlier, people who are culturally different from you may be put-off by too early use of questions. Self-disclosure on your part before questioning may be helpful in situations where cultures differ. With some reticent clients, some personal sharing helps generate more openness. Frank discussion of cultural differences may be useful. For example, "I'm White (or other background) and you are from a Mexican background (or other background). How does it feel to work with someone different from you?" "I'd appreciate your letting me know if you feel uncomfortable working with me at anytime. And let me know if I miss something." And, it is often helpful to say, "Do you have any questions for me? What might you like to know about me?" This provides the client with an opportunity to ask some critical questions and illustrates your own openness. Differences in race/ethnicity, gender, sexual orientation, and other issues are sometimes best discussed before the session gets fully underway.

LESS VERBAL CLIENTS AND OPEN AND CLOSED QUESTIONS

Generally, open questions are much preferred to closed questions in the interview. Yet, it must be recognized that open questions require a verbal client who is willing to share information, thoughts, and feelings with you. Following are some suggestions that may facilitate clients talking more freely with you.

Build trust at the client's pace. A central issue with hesitant clients is trust. If the client is required to meet with you or is culturally different from you, he or she may be less willing to talk. At this time, your own natural openness and social skills are particularly important. Trust building and rapport need to come first. With some clients, trust building may take a full session or more. Extensive questioning too early can make trust building slow with some clients.

Accept some randomness. Your less verbal client is not likely to give you a clear linear story of the problem. If he or she lacks trust or is highly emotionally involved in the concern, it may take some time for you to get an accurate understanding. You may need to use a careful balance of closed and open questions to draw out the story and get "bits and pieces" before you can put a coherent story together. Regardless of what you do, keep your language as simple, straightforward, and concrete as possible.

Search for concrete specifics. Counselors and therapists talk about the "abstraction ladder." If you or the client moves "too high" on the abstraction ladder, things won't make sense to anyone. This is especially so with less verbal or emotionally distraught clients. Constantly seek to find concrete examples and stories. Avoid searching for general themes and patterns. The open question, "Could you give me a *concrete, specific* example?" is a particularly effective general concrete question. Abstractions and repeating patterns of behavior, while important, should wait until the basic facts, feelings, and thoughts have been discovered.

Seek short, concrete answers. After some trust is generated, you might begin by saying, "The teacher said you and she had an argument." Then try asking the concrete open question, "What did your teacher say (or do)?" If you focus on concrete events and avoid evaluation and opinion in a nonjudgmental fashion, your chances for helping the client talk will be greatly expanded. You'd like to know what happened specifically, what each person said and did, and perhaps the accompanying emotions. Example concrete questions focusing on narrow specifics include:

> What happened first? What happened next? What was the result? (This helps you draw out the linear sequence of the story.)
>
> What did the other person say? What did he/she do? What did you say/do? (Focuses on observable concrete actions.)
>
> What happened after? What did you do after? What did he/she do after? (Sometimes less verbal clients are so focused on the event that they don't yet realize it is over. This helps them see the end and the consequences of the situation.)
>
> What did you feel/think just before it happened? During? After? What do you think the other person felt?

Note that each of the questions above requires relatively short answers. These are open questions that are more focused in orientation and can be balanced with some closed questions. Do not expect your less verbal client to give you full answers to these questions. You may need to ask closed questions to fill out detail and obtain specific information. ("Did he say anything?" "Where was she?" "Is your family angry?" "Did they say 'yes' or 'no'?")

The *leading* closed question is dangerous. In the examples above, you can see that a long series of closed questions can bring out the story, but it may be the client's limited responses to *your* questions rather than what the client really thought or felt.

Working with children. Children, in particular, may require considerable help from you before they are willing to share at all. With children, it really helps if you are naturally a warm, talkative person who *likes and accepts* children. Thus, it helps to begin sessions with children sharing something fun and interesting. Games, clay, and other toys in the counseling room are useful when dealing with children. You will find that children generally like to do something with their hands while they talk to you—drawing a picture during your conversation often is useful to them and to you. And, the drawings are often revealing as to what is going on in the child's life.

Summary. Your ultimate goal is to draw out: 1) the general picture of what happened ("could?"); 2) key facts of the situation ("what?"); 3) emotions ("how?"); and 4) where appropriate, draw out the reasons for the situation via the why question. *But do not expect this information to come in sequential order as above.* If you have patience and use attending skills well, you will eventually be able to bring out their full story. Clarifying skills (minimal encourages and paraphrases), reflection of feeling, and summarization, discussed in later chapters, will help you and the client organize the story more fully.

PRACTICE IN RECOGNIZING OPEN AND CLOSED QUESTIONS

The example interview below illustrates the varying types of questions. As you read the segment, classify each question as open or closed. Also circle the key words that indicate the type of question (for example, "Do," "Is," "What," "Why"). The following is a segment of an interview. Rapport and trust have already been established. The segment here starts with a summary of what the client has said previously. (Classification of Responses may be found at the end of this chapter.)

| | 1. Helper: | Cherilyn, so you say you are a single parent, that it has been hard for you at times, and that you would like to explore some issues about some difficulties with your children. |

1. Helper: Cherilyn, so you say you are a single parent, that it has been hard for you at times, and that you would like to explore some issues about some difficulties with your children.

2. Helpee: Yes, that's right. I've been a single parent for six years now.

_____ 3. Helper: Could you tell me a little bit about that experience? Maybe some frustrations that you may have had as a single parent?

4. Helpee: Oh, yes, there's been many. You'd think after six years, I'd really have it all together. You know, I have a career, I'm a counselor. And I have two daughters, and a decent apartment and all the usual things, and it's really hard balancing, trying to do everything, trying to be everything for my daughters, you know, helping them with homework, disciplining them, doing everything I was supposed to do. It's just difficult managing it all.

_____ 5. Helper: Cherilyn, I can sense it's a big task. Could you give me a specific example of one of the issues? (Comment: Using the client's name helps personalize the interview. Do try to use the client's name periodically throughout any session.)

6. Helpee: Well, I guess the thing that's bothering me most is that I am a counselor and I work with students and then I come home at the end of the day, and I see my own kids having such a difficult time getting along. They fight with each other, they hit each other, and they argue about everything, about clothes, about their friends, about the telephone, everything imaginable. And I just can't seem to be able to help them out and it's very frustrating.

_____ 7. Helper: Could you tell me about a specific situation where you had those difficulties? (Comment: Note that the helper has used three "could" questions in a row. The client is encouraged in each one to become more specific and clear.)

8. Helpee: Well, last weekend I took them out to buy school clothes. Then we stopped for lunch. A friend saw us and joined us.

Next thing the girls started pinching and poking and hitting and teasing right at the table. I didn't want to say anything because my friend was there, but I kept getting angrier with them.

_____ 9. Helper: Their behavior catches you by surprise. How old are the girls?
(Closed question useful for context—note that "how" and "what" questions can sometimes really be closed—"What age are they?")

10. Helpee: Well, they're eleven and thirteen. You'd think by that age they'd be able to handle themselves in public. And, it is starting to get violent.

_____ 11. Helper: Do they hit each other all the time, Cherilyn?

12. Helpee: Well, every day I'm sure. In fact endlessly, yes.

_____ 13. Helper: Have they been hit? (Comment: Ultimately, this is an important question to ask. Children who express violence often come from a violent home. Other useful, perhaps more indirect, questions here might have been "How do you react when they hit each other?" or "How do you feel about hitting as a way of discipline?")

14. Helpee: No, I don't hit them and that's why I can't understand why they hit each other.

_____ 15. Helper: Maybe they . . . Do you think they get it from their friends? Do their friends hit each other? (Comment: Here the helper has become trapped by closed questions. Closed questions can lead you to guessing what is in the client's mind and most of us aren't good "mind-readers.")

16. Helpee: I don't know. I'm confused.

_____ 17. Helper: Let's go back, Cherilyn. Earlier you said you were troubled by their behavior. Could you tell me more about that? (Comment: When things aren't going well in the interview, use a basic rule or attending behavior—go back to an earlier comment and ask an open question about that issue. Again, using the client's name respectfully is a useful adjunct to rapport and sometimes can get you through your errors. *It is not the mistakes we make that are so bad—all of us will make errors. What is important are our recovery skills!*)

18. Helpee: Yes, I was embarrassed. I know that the way one's children behave often reflects on what's going on at home. I worry about the interpretation that others are going to place on me. I don't hit my children, but I worry that others will think I do.

___ 19. Helper: Why do you think the children are hitting each other? (Comment: The potentially dangerous "why" question has been asked. It can put clients off, but if the relationship is good, sometimes useful information appears.)

20. Helpee: (breaks into tears and stammers) I think they are still reacting to the divorce. I do my best, but I can't manage them. My ex-husband used to hit us all.

In the example above you see a variety of questions used to bring out information from the client. Closed questions bring out specifics and open questions help clients explore more from their frame of reference. In this example, the helper got too involved in specifics at one point, but was able to salvage the situation. The helper did this through saying at 17. "Let's go back" and there he asked an open question about a previous topic. This is an example of how attending behavior (return to an earlier topic when you feel lost) helps you get started again.

As you gather data through open and closed questions, you can gradually learn the client's story and the client's plan for the future. Again with less verbal clients, pay special attention to focused questions that require shorter answers.

OPEN INVITATION TO TALK WITH FAMILIES AND GROUPS

Most family counselors and family therapists use questions extensively. The fast-moving and complex pace of the family session requires action on the part of the helper. Family sessions can easily swing totally out of control and the skilled use of questions provides you with powerful alternatives for action.

All of the questioning principles described in this chapter can be applied to family and group work. However, it is important to add the critical words "family" and "group" to at least some of your questions.

"Could you tell me something positive about this *family/group*? What seems to work well for you?"

"What's happening in the *family/group* right now?"

"How are you feeling right now about this *family/group*?"

"Why do you think this *group/family* is having this difficulty?"

In each of the examples above, the focus on the family or group helps each member to be aware that they are just that—a *member* of a group. Families and groups each have their own typical interaction style, rules, and norms that need to be examined.

PRACTICING OPEN INVITATION TO TALK

Again, it is your ability to use questions in your own helping interviews that is most critical. Here are specific suggestions for the practice session. You may want to refer to the earlier discussion of practice for attending behavior for more specifics.

1. *Develop a working group* of a pair, a triad, or four people.

2. *Assign roles for the practice session.*

    a. Helper

    b. Helpee

    c. Observer/operator

    d. Second observer

3. *Determine topic for role-play.* The suggested topic for this role-play is a *significant life event* such as divorce, marriage, death, obtaining a new job, an important dating experience, reactions to a new child, a significant success experience.

The task of the helper is to use open questions to bring out the facts, feelings, reasons, and the general experience via what, how, why, and could questions. A few closed questions should be used for variety. In addition, the helper should ask at least one question aimed toward specifics. "Could you give me a specific example?"

4. *Record interview and provide feedback.* Be specific and nonjudgmental.

5. *Rotate roles* so all participate.

GROUP/FAMILY PRACTICE IN OPEN INVITATION TO TALK

It is suggested that couple counseling be tried for this practice session.

1. *Develop a working group.*

    a. Two members become the couple

    b. Helper

    c. Observer/recorder

2. *Determine topic for role-play.* Any type of couple conflict is appropriate for this practice session.

3. *Planning.* The helper's task is to draw out the couple's conflict with as much information as possible. Ideally, the helper will want to know the facts of the situation as seen by each member of the couple, the feelings each has, and any reasons the couple can generate to explain what is occurring. The task is to draw out data and information, not to problem-solve.

    During planning time, the role-played couple can generate a tentative "script" concerning their "difficulties." The observer can study the observer form and prepare any recording equipment.

4. *Watch time carefully and provide feedback.* The role-play should last approximately 10–15 minutes. Allow 15–20 minutes for feedback.

5. *Rotate roles as time permits.*

OPEN INVITATION FEEDBACK SHEET

1. During each practice session, count the number of open and closed questions. As you make your counts, notice the response of the helpee to different types of questions. How long does the individual talk? What body movements do you notice in response to questions?

Session	Number of Closed Questions	Number of Open Questions
1.		
2.		
3.		
4.		

2. Was the helper able to use all four basic open questions? What was the result of each in terms of what the client said? Was a general picture of the problem brought out? Were the important facts and feelings discussed? Were the underlying reasons explored?

Could: _____

What: _____

How: _____

Why: _____

3. What closed questions were used and what was their impact on the client?

_____

_____

_____

4. Nonverbal observations of both helper and helpee's behavior.

_____

_____

_____

5. One specific suggestion for the helper to follow-up on would be:

_____

_____

DO-USE-TEACH CONTRACT

The **Do** portion of the contract is concerned with whether or not you actually can engage in a skill. Can you demonstrate attending behavior and questioning skills in an interview? The feedback sheets are concerned with your ability to engage in or *do* the skills.

The **Use** aspect of the contract is concerned with taking the concepts of the chapter out and *using* attending behavior, questions, and other skills in your daily life. What are some of the ways you can take the concepts of questioning out and *use* them to help you in your own daily communication? Generally speaking, the most effective *use* contract is to make an agreement with yourself or with your group to practice the learning of this chapter outside of the practice workshop and then report back what happened. This practice is what will make you an expert with the skill. Report below your own unique plan to use the skill of questioning and how well it worked for you.

USE: I plan to *use* open invitation to talk in the following context:

_____

_____

The result of my plan was:

_____

_____

The skills of this book are designed to be shared widely. Managers in business concerns, nurses and physicians, and other professionals use these same skills in much the same fashion as counselors and helpers. The context and content may vary, but the communication skills remain the same. Similarly, parents, children, teenagers, and others use these skills. They can profit from learning what you have learned. Thus teaching the skills of this book is an important aspect of your own training and the work of the effective helper.

The **Teach** aspect of Basic Attending Skills is critical. You will want to turn to the teaching methodology in Chapter 8 for more data and learn how to share what you know with others. The model of teaching communication skills suggested in this book is simple, but has been proven and tested through over 25 years of clinical training with hundreds of thousands of learners in fields as varying as counseling and law, medicine and community hot-line work, and the teaching of skills to parents and elementary children.

Also, recall that teaching attending behavior and questioning skills to clients may be a particularly effective treatment mode in its own right. It provides clients with useful social skills that they can use with their families, in their work, and in many other places.

The teaching model has been described in Chapter 1. To review:

1.   *Introduction/Warm-up.* When you teach the skill, provide a brief commentary or experiential exercise on what you are going to teach.

2.   *Reading about the skill.* Have the person you want to teach read information in the microcounseling manuals (particularly the first manual in each chapter).

3.   *Modeling.* You may want to demonstrate the skill yourself. You may want to develop your own audio or video training examples. It is most helpful to your trainee to see the skill in action.

4.   *Practice.* You'll then want to have the individual you are teaching practice the skill so that real mastery can be developed. You can serve as helpee and your student can be helper.

5.   *Generalization.* With your student, work on a way that they can use the Do-Use-Teach contract format.

Develop your own plans for teaching someone else the skill and summarize what happened in your own words in the space provided below or on a separate page:

Plan:

_____

_____

Result:

_____

_____

Classification of Responses

3. Open	7. Open	11. Closed	15. Closed	19. Open
5. Open	9. Closed	13. Closed	17. Open	

Nothing is more satisfying than being heard.

The minimal encourage helps you draw out the client's story.

The paraphrase shows the client that you have accurately heard their story and issues.

CHAPTER 4

CLARIFYING: THE MINIMAL ENCOURAGE AND PARAPHRASE

The skills of attending and questioning are useful in assisting the helpee to start talking. The skills of this chapter, the minimal encourage and the paraphrase, facilitate further conversation in more depth. These skills show the helpee that you have heard what has been said. When a person feels heard, they tend to build trust in the listener and are willing to say even more.

You will find that the minimal encourage is a most simple skill—yet it is one of the most powerful. The minimal encourage and the paraphrase both focus on using the key words of the client and then saying back to them the most important things they have said to you. At first glance, "saying back" what has been said sounds easy. However, selecting key words for encourages and accurate paraphrasing are two of the most difficult and important skills you can master.

The exercises and readings in this chapter will help you to:

1. Recall how you have felt when you have been heard and contrast that to when you were not heard. The two skills in this chapter are critical in helping clients to feel that you have listened to their stories.

2. Define the minimal encourage and paraphrase.

3. Distinguish how the paraphrase differs from the interpretation.

4. Demonstrate the two skills in a practice interview. In addition, you may wish to try the skills in a group or family situation.

5. Use the two skills in interviews and in your daily interactions with others. You will also be asked to consider yourself as a teacher of this skill both to clients and other helpers.

EXERCISE: WHAT DOES IT FEEL LIKE TO BE HEARD? NOT HEARD?

All of us have had times when someone didn't hear us. Perhaps you felt lost and lonely when someone didn't listen to a real concern or perhaps an important accomplishment was ignored. You have also experienced the joy of someone hearing you—it is a wonderful gift when someone truly listens to you. Take a moment and think of the importance of those times. The specifics of the event need not be written, but write below the feelings that occurred in each.

When someone listened to me, I felt: _____

_____

_____

When I wasn't heard, I felt: _____

_____

_____

With those feelings and thoughts in mind, we can examine the central skills of active listening—the minimal encourage and paraphrase. The minimal encourage and paraphrase are closely related. The first helps the client explore issues in more depth; the second facilitates accuracy of understanding and truly indicates to the other person that you have listened. Together these skills bring clarity to the counseling session.

THE MINIMAL ENCOURAGE: BASIC SKILL #3

Minimal encourages are small indicators to another person that you are with her or him. Once you have asked a question (or used any other counseling skill), you want to encourage the helpee to keep talking. You'll be surprised how very little in way of specific counseling leads are necessary if you just encourage the helpee to "keep going."

Nonverbal minimal encourages should be considered first. They are elaborations of attending behavior. For example, your client will talk more easily if you maintain culturally appropriate eye contact, your body leans forward with interest, and you use facilitative open gestures. Head nods are used by many counselors unconsciously and seem to facilitate talk.

In short, don't be wooden; find your own natural body style of encouraging others to share themselves with you. On the other hand, beware of awkwardness and moving too much. You'd like your body to be in tune with your client.

Verbal minimal encourages are brief utterances through which you can help the client move further or into more depth. Here are some useful examples:

1.   "Oh?" "So?" "Then?" "And?"

2.   "Umm-hummm." "Uh-huh."

3.   "Tell me more."

4.   The repetition of one or two key words.

5.   Simple restatement of the exact same words of the helpee's last statement.

Silence as a minimal encourage. On occasion the most valuable minimal encourage may be silence. Professional counselors talk about "response latency time" which means the number of seconds a helper waits before making a response. Many times the helper should give the helpee *time* to respond or to continue. The most classic example of inability to develop a satisfactory waiting period before continuing is the lecturer who finishes a point and then asks the group, "Any questions?" Before anyone has a chance to respond, the lecture continues.

Your own comfort level speaks in important ways to silence. If there is a quiet space in the session and you are uncomfortable, the client will sense that. If you indeed are uncomfortable, remember attending behavior. Focus on something the client just said and aim to pick out key words, perhaps repeating them as a minimal encourager.

The importance of restating key words: When single words or short phrases are repeated back to the helpee, they almost inevitably will respond by elaborating on the concept in more detail. One of the best ways, and least intrusive, to obtain further information and opinions from a helpee is to repeat back a key word or two or the exact same words of a short phrase. You may find that using a questioning tone of voice helps at times, for example, "sad and lonely?" Research shows that this type of minimal encouragement is used more and more by effective professionals and non-professionals as they grow over their careers.

Paraphrasing is closely related to the key word minimal encourage, but it focuses on what has been said and covers a longer time frame. In the paraphrase, you again want to use the client's key words as you say back to them the essence of their comments.

THE PARAPHRASE: BASIC SKILL #4

One of your most basic tasks is to *hear* the helpees clearly and to *let them know that they have been heard.* Accurately hearing and sensing another person is the basis for all the skills in this series. Paraphrasing is a special type of attending which demands that you demonstrate your ability to "give back" to that person what he or she has said accurately. Effective paraphrasing often implies a giving of self to another person to help him or her gain increased clarity on their issues.

Consider the following client statement:

> I've been having a terrible time with Susan. She just got promoted over me and she came on the job after me and I taught her how our systems work. She seems to have the big head. She's giving me a terrible time and keeps telling me what to do. I don't think anyone likes her.

Minimal encourage:	"Promoted over you?" (or "Terrible time?" or "Telling you what to do?" "No one?")
Paraphrase:	"Juan, you're saying that Susan was *promoted over you* and is giving you a *terrible time.*"

Note that the minimal encourage tends to lead Juan to elaborate in more detail on varying topics. The first leads to discussion of what happened over the promotion, the second focuses on Juan's difficult personal experience, while the third on other employees in the office. Each type of minimal encourage might lead Juan in a very different direction. By way of contrast, the paraphrase feeds back to Juan what he has been saying and indicates that he has indeed been heard. Note that some of the most important words that Juan used were repeated in identical form in the paraphrase, but that the interviewer/helper has shortened the statement, picking up the essence of what has been said.

The minimal encourage helps the client present more detail while the paraphrase indicates accurate listening. The paraphrase often leads to more detail, but it also serves to help a client move on to what he or she considers important.

The structure of the paraphrase should be considered. The most effective paraphrases consist of:

1. The client's name and/or the pronoun "you." There is clear evidence that personalizing the paraphrase makes it more effective.

2. The most important key words of the helpee.

3. A distilled, shortened, and clarified helper statement that catches the essence of what has been said.

The Check-Out: Occasionally, verify the accuracy of your paraphrases with the check-out, a closed question that gives the client a chance to react to your statement. Example check-out questions to follow your paraphrase are:

> Is that right? Am I close? Is that what you said? Am I hearing you accurately? OK?

If your paraphrase is successful, the helpee will likely reward you with words such as "exactly, " "yes," or "right." If the client needs to talk in more depth, the paraphrase facilitates more extensive talk. If the client has talked enough on a topic, the paraphrase facilitates movement to a new subject. There are clients who say the same thing over and over again. Paraphrasing can help them move on to other issues.

DISTINGUISHING PARAPHRASING FROM INTERPRETATION

In encouraging and paraphrasing we seek to help the client tell his or her story with minimal influence on our part. You want to hear how the client views a conflict, experienced a trauma, or thinks about a career decision. In listening, you want to hold back your ideas and interpretations and give the client prime attention.

Consider the following interviewing situation. Note that the three helping leads—minimal encourage, paraphrase, and interpretation—represent points on a continuum. The first two focus on the client's view of the situation. The interpretation focuses on the interviewer's view of the same situation and may bring a new meaning to the situation. Interpretations can be useful, but only after the client's story has been fully heard.

Helpee: I'm really feeling lost. My Dad drinks a lot and sometimes he beats my Mom. It's really tough at home. I find it really difficult to study or even do anything.

Helper: (Minimal Encourage) "You feel lost." or "Difficult to do anything."

(Paraphrase) "You're feeling *lost* because it's *really tough at home* and you can't *do anything.*" (Italics emphasize client's key words.)

(Interpretation) Sounds like your Dad is an alcoholic. That really makes it tough for any teenager.

Note that the interpretation may indeed be accurate, but it is the helper's viewpoint, and it may not be the client's. Helping theory holds that it is best if the client can come to the interpretation on his or her own. If you have worked with alcohol problems, you are well aware that naming a "drinking problem" as alcoholism is a big step. Thus, it is recommended that you first focus on the client's worldview through careful listening and save your interpretation until later.

Keep the following maxim in mind:

If you listen first,
clients are much more likely to accept your ideas,
advice, and interpretations later in the interview.

Even better, if you listen first,
many clients will develop useful
new interpretations and meanings on their own.

The above brief example should illustrate that defining the distinction between encouraging, paraphrasing, and interpretation is not an easy matter. Clearly in each case above the helper has *selectively attended to* what the helpee has said about the problem. The minimal encourage involves the helper minimally in what the client talks about while the paraphrase is the helper's effort to give back the essence (as the helper sees it) of what has just been said. The interpretation focuses on the helper's frame of reference rather than the client's view.

Paraphrases serve three purposes at this stage: 1) they convey to the helpee that you are with her/him, that you are trying to understand what is being said; 2) they crystallize a helpee's comment by making it more concise, thus helping give better direction to the interview; and 3) they provide a check on the accuracy of the perceptions of the interviewer.

INTEGRATING QUESTIONS, ENCOURAGES, AND PARAPHRASING

Basic Attending Skills are sequenced so that you can integrate the skills as each new dimension is added. For example, when you use the skill of questioning, you still need to continue culturally appropriate attending behavior. When you add encouraging and paraphrasing, questions can be integrated to facilitate client expression.

As clients tell their stories and talk about important life events, they develop new understandings which enable them to move on and sometimes even to rewrite their past history. Your task as a listener is to draw out the client's story as accurately as you can. It is the client's story and you want to keep your ideas and reactions out of the story.

Negative example. The first example below illustrates how your own interpretations can interfere with the client's story. As you read the counselor leads, classify each one as an open or closed question (O?, C?), minimal encourage (E), paraphrase (P), or interpretation (I). Also look for check-outs (C-O), which appear very similar to closed questions, but are clearly used for a different purpose. More than one counselor lead occurs in some of the statements. (See the end of this chapter for classifications of skills.)

_____ 1. Counselor: (To depressed client) What's going on with your family?

2. Client: They don't visit me at all any more.

_____ 3. Counselor: They don't visit you.

_____   Why do you think that is?

4. Client: They don't like me, I guess.

_____ 5. Counselor: Perhaps it's because you don't pay any attention to them.

6. Client: (defensively) Well, they don't pay any attention to me either.

As is common with many depressed clients, this client gives relatively short responses. There is a need to focus on specifics and encourage more concrete description.

Positive example.

_____ 7. Counselor: Alisia, you say that *they don't pay attention to you.*

_____ Could you tell me how it went the last time they came to see you? (Note the focus on concrete, specific events. This is useful with all clients, but particularly with less verbal clients.)

8. Client: It wasn't good. (Note that helper open questions don't always get long answers. With such clients, move to the search for concrete specifics.)

_____ 9. Counselor: *It wasn't good.*

_____ Could you give me a specific example of something that *wasn't good?* (It is important to use client key words in questions. This helps clients explore issues of underlying meaning in more depth.)

10. Client: Well, last time Mom didn't like the way I was wearing my hair. She had hardly got here, but that she was trying to get me to fix it like she wants it.

_____ 11. Counselor: Your Mom wanted you to wear your hair the way *she wants it.*

(Note use of client key words.)

	12. Client:	Yeah, she's always telling me what to do. It's almost easier to have nothing to do with her. (Small events between a client and parents often speak to and represent larger family issues.)
____	13. Counselor:	Alisia, I hear you saying that your Mom wanted you do things her way and it's easier for you to have *nothing to do with her.*
____		Is that right?
	14. Client:	Exactly, I just clam up and I don't say anything.
____	15. Counselor:	Uh-huh, *You clam up.*
____		Tell me more about what happens.
	16. Client:	I used to fight back when my Mom picked at me. Somehow I learned it is easier to just sit and do nothing and ignore her.
____	17. Counselor:	So, Alisia, I hear you saying you don't pay your parents much attention because you've found that it is *easier to sit back and do nothing.*

In the first example above, you have seen that clients can be "turned off" by interpretations of their situations. The second example focuses on the client's actual story of the visit. Through questioning, minimal encourages, and paraphrasing, the client's version of the story is brought out. Now that the story has been heard as the client wants to tell it, there is more possibility for working with the problem and finding a positive resolution.

Recall the following maxim:

> *The first step in helping clients change the meaning of stories, or their behavior, feelings, or thoughts, is to hear their story as they interpret it.*

Finally, note in the above example how the counselor used the major, key words of the client, whether using the minimal encourage or the paraphrase. Furthermore, questions that include key words of the client are also preferred.

USING THE CLARIFYING SKILLS WITH GROUPS AND FAMILIES

The minimal encourage and paraphrase are used with equal effectiveness with groups and in family work. You can bring out less verbal group or family members through focused and concrete open questions coupled with encouraging and paraphrasing. In such cases, the skills are used in much the same fashion as with individual work.

More difficult, but equally important, is using the paraphrase with the group or family as a whole. Here you need to use the key words "family" and "group" and paraphrase the essence of what all are saying. For example:

Mother: Sonya isn't eating. We're afraid she's bulimic.

Father: No, Mother, I don't think she is. She just wants to keep her weight down.

Counselor: Sonya? (Minimal encourage)

Daughter: I don't have any problem. Like Dad says, Mom's just making a fuss.

Counselor: The *family* seems to look at Sonya differently. Mom's worried about bulimia, but Dad thinks she's just trying to keep her weight down. Sonya thinks that Mom's just making a fuss. How do such differences of opinion get worked out in this *family?*

The example is obviously shortened. If you were working with an individual (and it could be Dad, Mom, or daughter), you would focus on how one person thinks. In family therapy and group work you have several individuals to respond to, but you also need to be aware of focusing on the group or family as a whole.

When paraphrasing what is happening in a group or family, you do much the same as you would with an individual, but you focus your helping statements on the group as a whole. A common family therapy and group technique is to ask each member of the group the same question and then to talk about how the family or group works on the question together.[1]

---

[1] Another useful technique is circular questioning. Here you ask one member of the group how she or he thinks another member would answer the question. Through using this type of questioning, you will often discover unsaid things in the group or family.

PRACTICING THE MINIMAL ENCOURAGE AND THE PARAPHRASE

1. *Develop a working group.*

2. *Assign roles* as helper, helpee, operator/observer, and second observer.

3. *Determine topic for role-play.* While any topic may be used, we have found talking about a family story is most useful. This can be the family of origin or the present living family of the client. The family story can be positive or negative, past or present. The task of the helpee is to use attending behavior and questions to bring out the story and then to use a variety of minimal encourages to keep the helpee talking and elaborating. At several points in the interview, the helper should paraphrase what the helpee has been saying, using the key words of the client.

4. *Watch time carefully and provide feedback.*

5. Rotate *roles.*

GROUP/FAMILY PRACTICE IN MINIMAL ENCOURAGES AND PARAPHRASING

It is suggested that structured group counseling be tried for this practice session. However, couple counseling or family counseling may be practiced as well if you prefer.

1. *Develop specific roles for the practice session.*

    a. Three or more individuals form the "group"

    b. Group facilitator

    c. Observer/recorder

2. *Determine topic for role-play.* Three possible topics for the group are: a) a current problem in ethnic or race relations in the community; b) problems which members might have in their work setting; c) future career plans of the group members.

3. *Planning.* The helper's task is complex in group work such as this. First, recall that your goal is to draw out individual and group stories, not problem resolution. Thus you would like to:

a.   Draw out each individual's story using questioning, minimal encourages, and paraphrasing.

b.   Find group themes. You will find that some members of the group tell similar stories and you can relate them together through paraphrasing. Furthermore, the group itself will have a style and you can use the key word *group* to help members look at the group interaction.

c.   Focus on the topic itself. Not only do individuals and groups have stories, but also you will find it possible to construct a joint picture of the problem or topic as the several individuals view it.

Group work makes it possible for (a) individuals to tell their stories; (b) see how their stories are similar to and different from others, and (c) learn more about the problem or topic.

4.   *Watch time carefully and provide feedback.* A meaningful group interaction will take at least 30 minutes and the same amount of time will be required for feedback and exploration of what happened. In the feedback session, give special attention to the role of the group facilitator.

RATING AND BEHAVIORAL COUNT SHEET FOR PARAPHRASING AND MINIMAL ENCOURAGES[2]

List the main words of each helper statement and indicate whether it is an open or closed question, minimal encourage, paraphrase, or other skill (O?, C?, ME, P, O). You will find that listing the main words of each helper statement will enable you to reconstruct the total session after it is completed even if you do not video or audiorecord.

With group or family practice, observers may also need to make brief notes of group and family members comments.

____ 1. _____

____ 2. _____

____ 3. _____

____ 4. _____

____ 5. _____

____ 6. _____

____ 7. _____

____ 8. _____

____ 9. _____

____ 10. _____

____ 11. _____

____ 12. _____

____ 13. _____

____ 14. _____

[2]Continue this format on a separate sheet of paper. You will find that maintaining records of individual, group, or family interviews will greatly facilitate your feedback sessions and your understanding of what happened. Use this feedback sheet as you practice other skills in this book as well.

DO-USE-TEACH CONTRACT

How are you going to use and teach these concepts?

Do In practicing and/or observing this skills I learned or noticed:

_____

_____

_____

Use I plan to use this skill outside this practice session as follows:

_____

_____

_____

Teach I plan to teach this skill to others as follows:

_____

_____

_____

_____

Classifications of Skills

1. O?	7. P, O?	13. P, C-O
3. E, O?	9. E, O?	15. E, E
5. Int.	11. P	17. P

*The artistic counselor catches
the feelings and emotions of the client.*

*Our emotional side often guides
our thoughts and actions, even
without our conscious awareness.*

CHAPTER 5

RESPONDING TO FEELINGS AND EMOTIONS

The most effective interviewers are gifted at entering the world of their clients, drawing out their stories, and understanding what has been said. *Empathy* is another word for this process. Your goal is to understand how clients see, feel, and hear the world around them. This is not your world, but you seek to enter the client's world without mixing in your own thoughts and feelings. Think of walking in another person's shoes, seeing the world as they see it, and experiencing their feelings, **but** you also manage to stay separate from them.

Basic to empathy are the listening skills of this book. However, many believe that the skill of reflection of feeling—the accurate sensing of the emotional world of the helpee—is the most important skill for developing empathic understanding. Emotions and feelings are at the core of our life experience.

The exercises and readings in this chapter will help you to:

1. Name emotions and understand their importance in the helping interview.

2. Define the skill of reflection of feeling and offer some practice in distinguishing it from other skills.

3. Examine some gender and multicultural issues around emotion. The skill of acknowledging feelings may be helpful in reflecting emotion to many clients.

4. Demonstrate the skill of reflection of feeling in a practice individual interview. In addition, you may wish to try the skill in family and group practice sessions.

5. Use reflection of feelings in your own interview practice and in daily life. You will also be encouraged to think about teaching this skill to others.

NAMING FEELINGS AND EMOTIONS

While many of us like to think that we make decisions rationally, in truth we aren't really satisfied unless the decision "feels good." Similarly, we may talk about our problems in an intellectual fashion, but unless we deal with the emotions underlying the issue, we are likely to continue old ineffective behavior. Talking about something does not necessarily mean that we are dealing with key underlying emotional issues.

For example, you may work with the child of an alcoholic family or with someone who experienced abuse. The facts of the situation may be clear, but the emotions may be buried. In cases such as this, your main task may be to uncover and help the client deal with complex, sometimes troubling and confusing emotions. Knowing that one should leave a bad relationship is one thing—having the emotional strength to do it is another.

Emotions are important in all helping relationships. The client may rationally choose a career, but later feel unsatisfied because emotional issues were ignored. The facts and the reasons for their decision may be clear, but until the client deals with underlying feelings about the job, something will remain unresolved. Most job problems are related to interpersonal and emotional issues rather than competence or ability to do the task.

Feeling words. As a first step toward responding to a client's feelings, you must be able to recognize and name those feelings. Some basic emotional states are listed below followed by some other related words. Extend that list yourself with even more words. The richer your feeling vocabulary, the more you will be able to understand the world of the client. Start with the basic "mad, glad, sad, scared."

Mad: anger, annoyed, hate _____

Glad: joy, happy, excited _____

Sad: misery, hurt, guilt _____

Scared: fear, worry, anxiety _____

Additional emotional words which fit in one or more of the above categories include: *relieved, exhausted, embarrassed, inadequate, indifferent, courageous, infatuated, tender*—the list of feeling words can go on and on. List as many additional feeling words as you can either here or on a separate page.

_____

_____

_____

Mixed feelings. Often your clients will present confused or mixed emotions. In many situations, we feel combinations of several emotions. We may be in love, but anxious about the result. We may be very pleased about a new job opportunity, but scared at the same time. Sorting out these mixed feelings is an important part of the helping process.

Some key examples indicating that a client has mixed feelings include the words *upset, torn, mixed up, confused, unsure, perplexed, troubled, and ambivalent.* These words are not themselves usually important underlying feelings. Rather, they often represent a surface description of deeper, complex feelings. A helpee may say that he or she is *upset* about a difficult relationship. If you listen further, you may find that the underlying feelings are *hurt, anger, rejection, but also remaining love and caring.*

When you hear words which represent complex, mixed feelings, reflect the surface word, but continue your listening to find underlying, more basic dimensions of emotion. Just reflecting back the key words "you feel torn" or "you were upset" may be enough for the client to elaborate emotions in more detail. On the other hand, questioning emotions can be helpful. For example, "You say you feel *torn.* Could you tell me more about what that word *torn* means to you?"

Feelings expressed as metaphor. Some clients will talk about feeling like a *"limp dish rag,"* that they have *"reached the bottom of the barrel,"* or perhaps they feel like *"a case of dynamite about to explode."* In each case, single words really can't express the depth of emotion. You will also want to be aware of metaphor as an important key to understanding the emotional world of your client. Metaphors are also like mixed feelings—there is more going on than just the surface expression.

Both verbal and nonverbal clients may find it easier to express their emotions via metaphor. Ask your client to imagine the way they feel and then to describe what it is like for them. Some of the most successful therapists and counselor work very effectively with metaphor. Metaphors could be described as the poetry of emotional life.

What are some emotional metaphors that occur to you?

_____

_____

_____

Nonverbal feelings. Be alert to the client's smile, the jiggling foot (which may indicate restlessness, anger, or boredom), and any form of body movement. Crossed arms or legs may indicate anger or defensiveness and wiping one's nose may indicate personal discomfort. Emotions are located in the body and careful observation of body movement will often give you better clues as to what is occurring in clients than the words they say.

Nonverbal feelings, however, are sometimes gender and culturally determined. Note body movements, eye contact breaks, etc., but always with some caution until you understand the meaning of the gesture or movement for the unique person from a unique cultural background.

Relating at the emotional level is difficult for many of us, as we have been taught in many cultures to control feelings. Yet, our feelings often obscure and confuse our thought processes. This very important skill of helping requires you to work hard to achieve both sensitivity to others and mastery of the skill.

REFLECTION OF FEELING: BASIC SKILL # 5

How can you help others to express the central concerns they are experiencing? One excellent way is to listen for and respond to the feelings of the client. Through reflecting feelings, you can facilitate the client's movement toward more complete self-acceptance and self-understanding. You would like to communicate to the client that you can accurately sense the world as he or she is feeling and experiencing it.

Most central to this skill is being alert to and responding to the *feeling* being expressed rather than the *content. What* the client is saying is the *content* portion of the message. You must also listen to *how* the client gives a message. For example, the client may speak more quickly when communicating enthusiasm, more slowly when communicating discouragement, etc. It is this *feeling* portion of the communication to which you are asked to give special attention.

In reflecting feelings, the following steps are most essential:

1. The feelings are named. This may be through the actual words used by the helpee, through metaphor, or through observation of nonverbal communication.

2. Begin sentences with phrases such as "You seem to feel . . . ," "Sounds like you feel . . . ," "I sense you're feeling . . . ," and add the labeled emotion.

3. The context may be paraphrased for additional clarification: "You seem to feel _____ when _____." or "You feel _____ because _____." Here we have a combined paraphrase/reflection of feeling.

4. If you are not sure of the emotion, add a check-out "Is that close?" "Is that the way you feel?" "Is that right?" This gives the client a chance to reflect on, add to, or correct your emotional reading.

Reflections of feelings are most often useful if immediate here and now feelings in the interview are labeled and worked through. Rather than working in the past tense ("You felt _____"), try to reflect present in-the-moment feelings ("Right now, you feel _____").

Let us expand on reflection of feeling with the acknowledgment of feeling and issues related to gender and culture.

ACKNOWLEDGING FEELINGS:
MULTICULTURAL AND GENDER CAUTIONS

Trust is important if your clients are to share their feelings with you. However, even in the most trusting relationship, some clients will have difficulty sharing and exploring their feelings with you.

For example, in most cultures, men are expected to hold back their feelings. You aren't a "real man" if you allow yourself to feel emotion. While many men can and do express their feelings in the helping interview, some should not be pushed too hard in this area in the first phases of counseling. Later, with trust, exploration of feelings becomes more acceptable.

In general, women in all cultures are more in touch with and more willing to share feelings than men. Nonetheless, this will vary with the cultural group. Some cultures (for example, Asian, Native American) at times pride themselves on their ability to control emotions. However, this may also be true with those of English or Irish background.

African-Americans and other minorities have learned over time that it may not be safe to share oneself openly with White Americans. In cross-cultural counseling situations, trust needs to be built before you can expect in-depth discussion of emotions.

The *acknowledgment of feeling,* a shortened form of the reflection of feeling, can be helpful with many men and clients who are culturally different from you. Rather than delve deeply into emotion, the helper simply notes the feelings briefly and moves on without further probing. The only real difference between a reflection of feeling and acknowledgment of feeling is that the acknowledgment occurs briefly in passing form whereas the reflection of feeling often becomes a major focus of the interview. For example,

Sounds like that made you angry. And what happened next?

It hurt you then. What happened just before?

In the examples above, the helper briefly acknowledges feelings and moves on.

Minorities, women, and gay people may experience discrimination, racism, sexism, or heterosexism as part of their daily life experience. If you are a majority person or a male, trust may be more difficult to generate with those different from you. Acknowledging the reality of discrimination and oppression and its personal and group hurt can be an important part of the trust building process. Similarly a minority person working with majority clients may expect some distrust toward them as well. The acknowledgment of feelings of possible distrust may be helpful if used carefully. For example,

Right now, you're not so sure that you want to share more on this. That's OK. Perhaps later. Let's go ahead. You were saying earlier . . .

For a client to share his or her emotional experience with you is an expression of trust. You must earn that trust with each client.

PRACTICE EXERCISES IN REFLECTING FEELINGS

In the examples below, you will have an opportunity to select statements that indicate you understand the client's feelings and internal emotions. Select the statement that would most likely evoke a client response of, "That's right!" Label each response as a question, paraphrase, minimal encourage, or reflection to feeling.

Helpee: So I'm wondering if you can help me find a new major. (pause) I suppose if I did find one, I'd just mess it up again. I just didn't do well last term.

Helper: a. You really want to find another major, but you're not sure it would work out.

b. You feel very discouraged right now, but you still have some hope for pulling it out.

c. You'd just mess things up again.

d. What majors are you considering?

e. Why do you feel that way?

In this first example, *b* is the only reflection of feeling. Note that a positive emotion as well as the negative has been reflected. Helper lead *a* is a reasonably good paraphrase, but ignores the underlying emotional aspects of the helpee's communication. *C* is a minimal encourager which may lead to more feeling discussion. Helper lead *d* is a question and tends to be a topic jump leading the helpee away from self-exploration into a new area. Finally, *e* is another question which does partially respond to feeling, but the "why" dimensions tend to put the helpee on the spot with a very difficult question to answer at this point.

Helpee:	What do you think I ought to do—run away, get a divorce, or just give in and take it? I feel so sad and lost.
Helper:	a. There just doesn't seem to be any way out!
	b. (Noting tears) You feel *really* sad right now.
	c. Are you thinking seriously of running away?
	d. (Silence)
	e. You're really concerned and troubled. It's really getting to you.

Example 2 has two possible reflections of feeling—*b* and *e*. Either could be appropriate. *B* is an accurate reflection and shows that the client has been heard. *After* hearing full emotional expression, the counselor can later bring in more supportive and helpful data. The temptation in moments like this is to comfort, give sympathy, and provide answers. We believe it best to allow full emotional expression before moving on. Response *a,* a paraphrase, might very well be as successful as the reflection of feeling as it seems to catch the essence of the client's state of being.

C by outward appearances would be an ineffective question, unless the context warrants it. The minimal encourager of silence might be very effective, but of course is not a reflection of feeling. Response *e* is another reflection and may be useful. It does not seem to go into as much depth as *b*, but may be more appropriate depending on the immediate situation. In reflecting feelings, it often helps to use the major feeling words of the client even though you might add other words as well.

Helpee:	You know, it's funny, but when I talk to you, I just feel shaky. It's the silliest thing!
Helper:	a. Are you anxious in many situations?
	b. You wonder why you do this.
	c. Right now you feel very shaky talking to me; it confuses you to feel that way.

    d. Could you share a little more about how you feel toward me?

    e. You're laughing as you tell me you feel shaky and scared.

The final example has two reflections of feeling, *c* and *e*. *C* has the advantage of here and now immediacy, *e* the advantage of pointing out the mixed messages of feelings. Question *a* may be a good approach *if* the feelings have already been explored and are known and acknowledged; it does respond to emotion and gives the client room to explore. It would be unwise, however, if this is new information.

Question *d* has immediacy and gives the client room to explore emotion, thus underlining the fact that one need not stick exclusively to reflections to help others express their emotions. Questions, however, still do not fully acknowledge the experience of the helpee. *B* impresses us as a poor minimal encourage, but even this response could be good *if* the counselor's vocal tone is warm and supportive. Your personhood may be more important than what you say.

The above examples illustrate an important point. *No single response is going to be "right" or "wrong."* What you want is to have several alternatives available. We obviously favor, at this point, the reflective listening skills—especially giving special attention to feelings. At other times you'll find advice, interpretation, and other skills useful with your clients. It is your ability to have many possibilities in reserve that will enable you to reach many clients.

SORTING OUT COMPLEX MIXED FEELINGS

Very few of us have what we might call "pure" emotions. Our emphasis thus far has focused primarily on identifying and reflecting single emotions.

What are mixed or ambivalent feelings? All of us experience them daily, some of them produce deep conflict and problems difficult to resolve. Here are some common situations that we all face:

An examination is coming up which is very important. Your best friend suggests a movie.

    The mixed feelings underlying this decision might include *enjoyment* of movies, *fear* of failing the exam, *boredom* with studying, *caring* for your friend, etc. Resolution of even a simple decision such as this can be facilitated by exploring the many rich and varied emotional factors.

You face a major conflict with a loved one.

The mixed feelings here may include positive feelings of *caring, love, and trust.* The negative feelings *(hurt, anger, fear)* conflict with the positive. Sorting out such mixed feelings is often a basic goal of counseling.

Often complex feelings are hidden by words such as "confusion," "torn," and "ambivalent." If a client says he or she is confused, it is important to use questions and reflection to discover the more precise feelings underneath the vague term of confusion. Too often counselors and interviewers settle for the feeling of confusion and fail to find the underlying complex emotions.

How does a helper cope with the wealth of emotion underlying key decisions? The beginning is reflection of identified feelings plus focused questions that help the client explore emotional experience.

Useful skills in facilitating this exploration are:

1. Noting of double messages and mixed feelings. The body might say one thing while the words say something else. For example, "You sound like you are very sure of yourself, but your body seems to be giving a different message." This lead, of course, is best reserved for those clients who are aware of body language and its meaning. It does no good to reflect emotions that the helpee will only deny.

2. Questions, which provide openings for the individual to share more emotional experience in words. "What are your feelings?" "What's going on in your body as you say that?" "How did you feel when that happened?"

3. Reflections of feeling which name the mixed emotions.

4. Checking-out the client's reaction to your reflection. "Is that close to the way you feel?" "Does that make sense?"

More than one emotion is shown in the following examples. Name the emotions and then write how you might respond to them. Use reflections, questions, and the check-out to help clients explore their underlying emotions.

Client: Things have been going better with my husband's drinking lately, and I'm feeling more hopeful. But my friends at Alanon (support group for families of alcoholics) worry me. They say it's only a phase.

What feelings do you note? _____

How would you respond? _____

_____

Client: (Having just gone through the breakup of a long-term relationship.) It's been such a struggle to become independent, and I've waited so long. I guess I didn't anticipate the feeling of loneliness that it was going to bring.

What feelings do you note? _____

How would you respond? _____

_____

Client: Gee, I really feel confused. One side of me says, hey, let's move to that new job. It's exciting and challenging. The other side of me feels afraid. And I end up just feeling torn and confused, I'm not sure what I want.

What feelings do you note? _____

How would you respond? _____

_____

TRANSCRIPT OF REFLECTION OF FEELING

Making decisions is not always a rational process. The emotions and feelings underlying the decision often determine what the person decides. In the following brief example you will find that the rational facts of an important job decision are less impactful on the final decisions than the underlying emotions.

The following transcript is particularly effective in its use of reflection of feeling. As you classify the helping leads, you will discover extensive use of the skill. In addition, note the way that questions are often focused on exploration of feelings and you will even find some minimal encourages which focus on feelings. In cases where reflections and paraphrases are combined, note them both in classifications. Classify leads as O?, C?, ME, P, and RF. Note the check-out with a CO. (See the end of this chapter for classification of listening skills.)

_____ 1. Helper: Could you tell me about your new job opportunity?

2. Client: Well, Helper, it's really an exciting one. It's in another state and the colleagues are absolutely fantastic, the salary is a lot better than I have. And I certainly could use the money.

_____ 3. Helper: You sound really excited about it.

4. Client: I really am. It's really just like I feel the opportunity of a life-time. Really the opportunity of a lifetime. But . . . ? Even as I talk I sort of say, wow, I'm not quite sure what that would mean. A long way from here, gee, the kids are here and in college and I'd like to be with them and that's a long way away.

_____ 5. Helper: You sound sort of hesitant—anxious about it? (_The questioning tone of voice serves as a check-out. Here the helper has given the emotional word to the client._)

6. Client: Exactly, and I really do get anxious because the opportunity is fantastic and yet, there are a lot of things holding me here too. For example, you know, I mentioned the kids, I've made a lot of friends. I like the people I work with, I don't have any real strong . . . nothing really pushing me away, it's more an

exciting new challenge. And yet, the thought of leaving where I am, it does make me feel very anxious.

The next helper lead summarizes what has been said so far. You are asked to classify the three parts of the summary. The summary will be discussed in the next chapter.

_____ 7. Helper: As I hear you saying, you've talked about the excitement about moving, a new challenge, the people you'll be working with and that sounds very exciting.

_____ And on the other hand, you've got some nice things going here. You've got colleagues that you've worked through lots of relationships with, and you understand them. Finally, you've got your kids here.

_____ And so there's kind of confusion between the two, and you know, what looks better. The excitement out there or your feelings for your family and your comfort here. Am I hearing you accurately? (*The mixed feelings around the decision are confronted.*)

8. Client: You sure are. What I'm sure of here is that I do like to go to work; I find the people I work with compatible, I find them interesting, I like the students. I certainly love New England, and that's certainly a major plus. It's fall now and it really feels pretty good, really nice. At the same time New England has certain problems. The economy is ghastly. I get very frustrated and angry with the fact that there's never enough time and money to do what I want to do.

_____ 9. Helper: Frustrated and angry about . . . ?

10. Client: Well, for example, frustrated and angry in terms of, like, I find myself trying to do a good job, but worrying that the job may not exist in a year or so. The economy just doesn't seem very promising.

_____ 11. Helper: So you're wondering if this move . . . if now's the time to make the move?

_____ What has been your experience with moving in the past? And how have you felt when you moved?

12. Client: Well, that's helpful. When I first . . . the first major move I made was from Pennsylvania to Colorado, and that was an absolute up. I just felt that anytime I could move, I could leave all the mistakes behind me, and you know me, I had plenty of mistakes! As I got to Colorado . . . and I just fit in, wonderful time, loved it professionally. It just was really a real high professionally at least.

_____ 13. Helper: So that first move was excellent, and it was exciting, wonderful.

14. Client: Really exciting. It was really good.

_____ 15. Helper: And then what happened?

16. Client: And then I moved to New England and when we arrived here, nobody basically spoke to us for the first six months. New England's a great place but it takes a long time to get in.

_____ 17. Helper: So you felt a little lonely when you first got here?

18. Client: You really caught it! It was absolute agony. And I mean literally even now at this moment, it almost brings tears to my eyes about leaving those people I cared so much about in Colorado. And now . . . and it took me, I'd say four years before I felt comfortable here.

_____ 19. Helper: So it took you a long time to settle in here and you're maybe thinking that it might take a long time to settle in a distant new state. You seem to feel anxious about this. Is that close to what you think and feel? (_Note that while emotions are central in this example, the facts of the situation remain important._)

20. Client: I don't only think, I know, and the thought of leaving my kids here is not good, because they wouldn't be coming to visit as often.

_____ 21. Helper: How would that make you feel?

22. Client: It's terrifying, because maybe I wouldn't be that much ahead financially. And just that whole pain of separation and then starting again with new people would be really overwhelming.

_____ 23. Helper: So you're wondering if the pain is worth all the excitement of the new job, that even though there'll be an exciting new job and a new challenge, with all the pain, would it be worth it? You know, in terms of the pain. The trade-off. (*This also is a summary as it integrates much of what has been said so far.*)

24. Client: And at this moment, as I start balancing, maybe it isn't worth it.

This transcript is presented as it illustrated clearly the importance of underlying emotions. You will find that often your clients come to you with little awareness of how important emotional experience is in their decision-making and total life process. Focusing on and reflecting feelings can be an invaluable part of the counseling and therapy process. Reflecting feelings can be helping at its best.

REFLECTION OF FEELINGS IN GROUP AND FAMILY INTERVIEWS

Family problems often rest on a sometimes explosive foundation of emotion. The problem with the family may be presented rationally and clearly and yet you can sense the strong feelings underneath. The same applies to group sessions. Individuals present issues, then you find what they are *really* feeling as the group progresses.

Not only do members of families and members of groups have feelings, but there is also a joint "feeling tone" which is not the feelings of any one member, but speaks to the whole group. For example, you may work with a group who does not know each other well. The various members may be expressing themselves clearly, but underlying disagreements or emotions may be buried. Your task as a group leader or family counselor is to help the members examine deeper emotional issues in a safe fashion.

In group and family work you will want to acknowledge and reflect individual feeling. In addition, you may also want to focus your reflections on the total group or family itself through questions oriented to emotion, minimal encourages, and reflection of feeling.

> This *family/group* seems to have something unsaid right now? What do you think it is?

> There seems to be tension in the air for all of us right now. What is the *group/family* feeling?

> This *group/family* has been sitting here for awhile. What emotions and feelings seem to represent this *group/family?*

> What was the impact of what was just said on the *group/family?*

> The *group/family* seems (sad, glad, relieved, angry, etc.) right now.

Note that the skill remains the same, but the focus turns to the total group or family. As in all other listening skills discussed in this book, reflection and exploration of feelings that focus on the group as a whole can be especially valuable.

PRACTICING REFLECTION OF FEELING

1. *Develop a working group.*

2. *Assign roles* as helper, helpee, operator/observer, and second observer.

3. *Determine topic for role-play.* It is suggested that the helpee talk about a time which involved some type of separation from loved ones. Important separations in life include leaving home for work or education, one's own breakup of a relationship or the divorce of one's parents, the death of a loved one, children growing up and leaving home. There are many important separations we face over the life cycle. These separations often form an important part of the issues that you will face in helping relationships.

A note to the helpee—you must be emotionally expressive or it will be very difficult for your helper to reflect feelings.

Give special attention to complex, mixed emotions. If you hear vague feelings such as "confused," "torn," or other ambivalent messages, use questions to help sort out the deeper feelings underneath. You will find yourself naturally including reflection of feeling with the paraphrase.

4.   *Watch time carefully and provide feedback.*

5.   *Rotate roles.*

GROUP/FAMILY PRACTICE IN REFLECTION OF FEELING

It is suggested that family counseling be tried for this practice session.

1.   *Develop a working group.*

a.   Three members become the family.

b.   Helper

c.   Observer/recorder

2.   *Determine topic for role-play.* Family problems often arise during key times of separation during the life cycle. The couple may be divorcing, moving to a new location, a child may be leaving home for college, a grandparent may be moving in, one of the parents may have lost a job, or any one in the family may be seriously ill.

3.   *Planning.* The helper's task is to draw out the family separation issue, but pay special attention to individual feelings. Ideally, the helper will want to know the interpretations and feelings around the separation situation as seen by each member of the family. The task is to draw out data and feelings, not to problem-solve at this time.

The helper should look for a general family feeling tone. How is this family functioning, as a whole unit, at an emotional level?

During planning time, the role-played family can generate a tentative "script" concerning their separation issue. The observer can study the observer form and prepare any recording equipment.

4. *Watch time carefully and provide feedback.* The role-play should last approximately 10–15 minutes. Allow 15–20 minutes for feedback.

5. *Rotate roles as time permits.*

RATING AND BEHAVIORAL COUNT SHEET
FOR REFLECTION OF FEELING

1. During the practice session, list the emotions you observe in the helpee or family/group—both verbal and nonverbal.

_____

_____

2. List each reflection of feeling used by the helper. Use exact words as closely as possible. How well do they match the feelings listed in #1 above?

_____

_____

_____

_____

3. List observations of non-verbal behavior.

_____

_____

_____

_____

4. Cite one strength of the interview and one specific area on which the helper might want to improve. Be as direct and clear as possible.

_____

_____

_____

_____

5. If a second observer is available, record each helper statement. In this way the content of the session can be readily reconstructed.

_____

_____

_____

_____

A DO-USE-TEACH CONTRACT

Do: I did use reflection of feelings during the practice sessions (when, where, and with what effect?):

_____

_____

_____

Use: You will find it interesting and helpful to practice acknowledging feelings in your daily life—at restaurants with a busy waitperson, with clerks in the store, with busy co-workers on the job, even with family members. There are many emotions you encounter constantly.

I plan to use this new skill outside this session in the following manner:

_____

_____

_____

Teach: At this point in the book, you may want to think about how you could help train peer counselors or family members in listening skills. Naming and reflecting feelings is an important part of any such training.

My plans to teach this important skill to someone else are as follows:

_____

_____

_____

Classification of Listening Skills

1.	O?	9.	E	17.	RF
3.	RF	11.	P, O?	19.	P, RF, CO
5.	RF	13.	RF	21.	O?
7.	RF, P, RF-CO	15.	O?	23.	P, RF

*To summarize, put the client's
thoughts, feelings, and behaviors
together accurately.*

*Not only will the client feel heard,
but also you will understand
what the client has been saying more fully.*

CHAPTER 6

SUMMARIZATION: INTEGRATING CLIENT BEHAVIOR, THOUGHTS, AND FEELINGS

Summarization is a rather straightforward skill. Doing it well, however, is another matter. This skill is similar to the paraphrase and reflection of feeling, but requires deeper concentration on helpee statements over time. It also requires you to synthesize a number of client statements into a more integrated whole.

You will find that summarization is a particularly valuable skill, both to you and to the client for it helps us understand what is actually being said more completely and fully. For example, many clients "talk around" their problems, but through careful listening you gradually begin to understand what is really going on. Through summarizing the "bits and pieces" of what a client has said, both you and the client gain important understandings of complex issues, concerns, and client problems.

The exercises and readings in this chapter will help you to:

1. Understand how the skill of summarization helps organize interviews and client thinking about problems.

2. Define the skill of summarization.

3. Demonstrate the summarization skill in a practice interview, and consider its implications for family and group interviews.

4. Use summarization in your daily practice of interviewing, and consider how you might teach this important integrative skill to others.

SUMMARIZATION AND ITS IMPORTANCE IN ORGANIZING INTERVIEWS

The clients who come to you are often confused. They may have so many things going on in their lives that they don't know which way to turn. They may experience mixed emotions. Important facts regarding decisions may be overlooked. At other times, you may work with clients who seem very organized, but actually are rigid and missing important parts of their own daily life.

One of the major tasks you face as a helper, counselor, or therapist is to help clients organize themselves, clarify thinking and feelings, and in the process learn how to look at themselves more clearly. When we use summarization, we recapitulate, condense, and organize the essence of what clients have said.

The skill of summarization involves listening to a client over a period of time (from three minutes to a complete session or more), picking out relationships among key issues, and restating them back accurately to the client.

By using summarizations periodically, we can check out our perceptions with helpees to see how accurate our listening has been. Also, this skill aids helpees in seeing their own personal distortions. By accurately condensing what has been said, we offer helpees a chance to examine their own thinking.

In the space below, you may want to brainstorm or list some examples where you have felt disorganized. This could be in your own personal life or even in your own past work as an interviewer.

_____

_____

_____

_____

SUMMARIZATION: BASIC SKILL #5

Summarization is not often identified as a skill used in counseling. We are prone to think of attending behavior, reflection of feelings, the use of questions, and paraphrasing as the essential dimensions of listening skills. Yet, it is summarization that brings together information gained via these other skills and helps the client "pull it all together."

The key purpose of summarization is to help another individual integrate behavior, thoughts, and feelings. A secondary purpose is to check on whether or not you as helper have fallen into distortion. When a summarization is accurate and without distortion, it can help move the interview from exploration to action and problem solving. A good summarization provides a crucial lever, indicating to the helpee that you have heard the entire story thus far.

Summarizations are similar to paraphrases and reflections of feeling. A summarization of feeling is close to a reflection of feeling with one major exception: a summarization of feeling covers a longer time period and involves a broad range of feelings that the helpee has expressed. A summarization of content is similar to a paraphrase, but differs in the same respect. The time period covered by a summary is longer. A paraphrase deals with the client's last few sentences or a short paragraph. A summary puts together a number of client paragraphs, an entire session, or perhaps even issues expressed over a series of several interviews.

Usually, we do not distinguish between a summarization of feeling and a summarization of content. This is because you usually want to integrate *both* emotions and content in your interviewing practice. The distinction between summarization of content and summarization of feeling remains useful, however, as it reminds us that we need to think of both dimensions when we help clients integrate their thinking.

Examples of Summarization

The following summarizations cover both emotional and objective content:

To a helpee who is struggling with a difficult employer and has been told of a possible layoff.

As I understand what you have been saying over the past hour, there seem to be three key things: 1) you're very angry and hurt at what's being done to you; 2) nonetheless, you feel that you need and want to look at what you can do to improve your job performance; and 3) as we've talked, it sounds like you would like to meet again next week to work on that. *Have I heard you accurately?*

To a parent troubled by a son taking drugs (third session of a continuing series):

You now seem to be feeling very aware that your control of your son, making him "toe the line" on every issue, may have been overly harsh and one of the reasons he joined the drug scene. This contrasts with your feelings of anger the first time we met when you said that the school was at fault. You also seem to be saying that you "gave up" on him too soon and now want to take a new, more balanced approach. *Is that right? Have I missed anything?*

In each of the examples above, the helper gives back to the helpee the essence of what has been said while exploring both cognitive and emotional dimensions of the problem. Before moving on, note that the check-out is especially important so that you can see if you have heard accurately and not distorted the message.

Specific behaviors and things to think about as you summarize:

1. Use questions, minimal encourages, paraphrases, and reflections of feeling, to indicate to the helpee that you are attending and with her/him.

2. Note important behaviors, thoughts, and feelings throughout the interview. Look for repeating patterns. Also, search for inconsistencies in feelings or facts. Most people have mixed feelings toward important people or situations and reflecting to the helpee these mixed feelings may be especially valuable.

    At other times, you will find your client telling you two different stories in the same session. Summarization helps you and the client clarify what has happened.

3. When the helpee is making a decision, give special attention to central threads of information throughout the session. Note the main issues so you can give them back later.

4. At several points during the session, time your comments appropriately and summarize for the helpee what you have heard so far.

5. Include frequent checkouts to ensure accuracy of hearing.

The summarization skill may be helpful to:

1. Begin an interview ("You said you wanted to see me about _____." "In our last session we talked about _____.")

2. Clarify what is happening, particularly when the interview is particularly complex ("Could we stop for a moment and see where we are to this point?")

3. Provide smooth flow from topic to topic during the interview ("So far you've been saying _____. Now what's on your mind?").

4. Bring together what has been happening in the interview over the entire period of an interview ("Today, we talked about _____").

5. Bring together threads of data over several interviews ("Last week you said _____ and today you say _____").

TRANSCRIPT OF SUMMARIZATION IN ACTION

You will now examine an interview that demonstrates summarization. Ordinarily, one does not summarize as frequently as illustrated in this example, but when you have a highly verbal client, you will find it helps both you and the client to summarize frequently. Otherwise you may become confused by the client's complex message. You will also find that good summaries help stop the client from saying the same thing over and over again.

The following interview is from the second session. You will find that the counselor is very active, but is constantly bringing data together in summaries as she challenges the client to respect what she, the client, really wants.

Again, classify the counselor's leads with O?, C?, E, P, RF, and S. Give special attention to the check-out (CO). In the counselor's leads below, give special attention to distinguishing between a combined reflection of feeling/paraphrase and the summarization. Recall that the summarization covers several statements and longer period of time. (See the end of this chapter for skill classifications.)

1. Counselor: Jaylene, the last time we were talking, I recall you talked about being a single parent and that requires organizing your time. You also are proud of your recent masters in business, although it was quite a struggle to do that while you worked as a teacher. *(Classify #1 and 3 together. They represent a single skill.)*

2. Client: (Interrupts) Oh, yes, for sure.

_____ 3. Counselor: And you have an enormous responsibility in raising children between that and your career, there is not much time for a personal life. And you're saying, how do I get all that together? Given that, what would you like to focus on today?

4. Client: I guess I would like to talk about my career. I've been feeling like I haven't been going any place; like I'm at a standstill. You know I went on in the midst of a separation and divorce and did get a masters degree in business and I'd like to move to that area. As a teacher, I've done some consulting and some workshops and I seem to be able to do it right within the school system, you know, I don't venture out too far. I've been reasonably successful, but I just can't seem to make that break from moving from teaching into something else, into consulting, or perhaps into business. I'm trained to work in the area, but somehow I'm kind of afraid to move.

_____ 5. Counselor: So on one hand here, you are feeling good that you've accomplished all this, getting your degree and you ought to be moving forward and doing something different; and on the other hand, it's fairly comfortable sitting where you are with the present job you've got. Have I got that straight?

6. Client: Yes, it's very comfortable. I like the people I'm working with and the schedule; it matches my children's schedule. I have the same holidays they do, and the same summer vacations and when you're a single parent, that's important. I can be with them and help them with their activities and homework and all those kinds of things. I'm kind of afraid though if I move away from education and go into business, I would be much busier. You know, it would be eight to five and weekends perhaps and two weeks vacation. That's a big change for me, from teaching.

_____ 7. Counselor: Well, are you saying that if you leave the school system, the responsibility of taking care of your children is such that you can't take on the responsibility of a new job? And that it's probably going to be more demanding. *(Note, the question mark after "job?" does not indicate a question. Rather, helpers often raise the tone of their voice at the end of a paraphrase, reflection of feeling, or summarization with an implied question. This questioning tone functions much like a check-out, but is not classified. Do not confuse questions with a questioning tone of voice.)*

8. Client: Well, I'm kind of worried about whether or not I can handle all that responsibility. I can barely hold it together as it is now. But money is tied in there too, because as you know, education is not the place to be these days. I mean you don't make a lot of money when you're working in school systems and I would be able to make more money if I moved out and did some things in business. But, you know, it's like . . . you know, the trade-offs are there all the time. I just don't know if I can make it in a new field.

_____ 9. Counselor: So, in other words, there are the successes that you've had in your career, the success that you've had in bringing up your children, suddenly the . . . really the heavy money burden is getting more so with the economy where it is now. And now you're faced at a point where you want or have to make a change.

_____ And what's going to happen to you and your family if you make that change?

10. Client: Yes . . . Well I think it might be an upheaval for my kids and for myself . . . it will be a whole change in our lifestyle and things have been going fairly smoothly, and fairly successfully, and you know, I'm afraid to rock the boat. Yet, on the other hand, I'd like to try some new things.

_____ 11. Counselor: Let me throw something out to you. If you were a man, and faced with this dilemma, what do you think would happen?

12. Client: Well, I think men are trained to move up the hierarchy just a little bit easier. I mean, they just take those risks and they move up, and I think women, you know, aren't trained that way. We're looked to be successful if we raise our kids and the kids turn out pretty well and if we hold a reasonably competent job, then we look pretty successful. And I don't know.

_____ 13. Counselor: I hear you talking about women, but are you describing yourself? *(The client has talked in general terms about women. The counselor asks her to focus on herself.)*

14. Client: Yes, I think right now I look pretty successful in the eyes of a lot of other women and a lot of my friends. And I'm not sure I'd find that same success out in the business world.

_____ 15. Counselor: So there is something in the fear of a failure at this point? *(Again, the questioning tone of voice.)*

16. Client: Right, a fear of failure, and not being so successful.

_____ 17. Counselor: Jaylene, let's go back to what does success mean to you?

18. Client: Well, I think it is important that my kids turn out well and that is very important. I'm very proud of their accomplishments so far. I think it's important to be personally satisfied, perhaps satisfied in a career. It's important to be financially independent or responsible enough that I can manage things without too much difficulty, and of course that's a big thing right now. I also would like to, you know, just push myself a little more. Push myself to those limits and see what those limits are. That sort of gets in the way of all these other things.

_____ 19. Counselor: Let me summarize again. One, it's important for you to be a good parent, the other, it's important for you to have a career, the other, it's important . . . the economics is important. But there's another thing that I heard, that maybe you'd like to push yourself. You know, maybe take a chance. And maybe you think that . . . or maybe it would be helpful for us, for you to focus on maybe yourself, personally, and not that the others aren't important, but why don't we focus on you, Jaylene, and where you're going to go?

20. Client: What I'm going to do with my life, you mean?

____ 21. Counselor: Several times, Jaylene, I've asked what you want. You seem to focus on other's needs and seem to find it very hard to speak about what you want. One of the things that I'm picking up is that you're not willing or anxious to look at what you really want even though we are talking about it right now. You really don't feel it's time to think of just Jaylene. Am I hearing you correctly?

22. Client: I'm afraid you're right. I guess I don't.

____ 23. Counselor: You're afraid I'm right.

24. Client: You know it's hard for me to get an image of what I would be beyond what I'm doing now. Well, maybe, you know, having a job with more responsibility, being in contact with more adults, maybe doing something new. It's real hard for me to get a handle on that. I don't know. I don't see any models out there of what I want to be like. I've seen a lot of models of what I'm like right now, but I don't see the other. It's very hard to imagine it.

____ 25. Counselor: It's hard to imagine. So far, I'm hearing very much that you'd like to move on and use your masters degree? I hear that you feel good about what you've done professionally and personally. And I hear you struggling now with the desire to move toward some action. Am I hearing you right?

26. Client: Exactly, I think I need to talk more precisely about getting out and looking for a new job. It sounds like I'm spinning my wheels again and again. My kids are getting older and perhaps we could manage the change.

You will often work with clients who present diffuse, confused thinking on complex topics. They need help in organizing the major issues and clarifying their thinking. The example above is fairly representative of verbal clients who are trying to take many factors into account in making a major decision. You will also work with less verbal clients who have even more complex decisions to make. Here again, the ability to summarize and bring data together is a most important skill.

SUMMARIZATION WITH FAMILIES AND GROUPS

In some ways, the summarization skill is even more important in group and family counseling. Not only do you need to summarize what occurs with each individual, you also need to be able to summarize the many complex interactions of the family or group. Some might argue that the summarization skill is second in importance only to questioning skills when you work with groups. Certainly, summarization is a skill that can help groups and families build better understanding and more harmonious relationships.

The following are some specific types of summarizations that can be useful in group and family interviewing.

1. *Beginning or ending a session.* It is especially helpful to a group if the helper summarizes where they were in the last session or what happened during a session. This provides you with an opportunity to include everyone, make observations on group interaction, and highlight important issues.

2. *Summarizing sequences of conversation or behavior.* Often you will see a family or group in which certain people speak first and then others either agree or disagree in a continuing sequence. It helps a group to look at itself when you point out, for example, "Father just reprimanded Jennifer. Jordan then moved closer to his Dad. Mother comforted Jennifer. I've seen this pattern several times today. What do you make of it?"

3. *Summarizing diverse points of view or issues of conflict.* You can be on the spot in family counseling or in group sessions. If you summarize what each person has said, you have shown ability to hear everyone equally. This supports each group member, gives you some neutrality in complex situations, and helps the group look at its own process.

4. *Summarizing group process.* A major distinction between individual and group/family work is a focus on what is happening among members. Almost any type of summarization in which the words "family" or "group" are used (instead of individual observations) represents this type of summarization. For example,

> This group has a pattern of starting slowly.

> This seems to be a family that is very careful of protecting its members.

> This group seems to enjoy conflict.

> This family appears to need conflict to hold it together.

Each of these summary statements needs to be amplified by examples, but at times, the one-line summary above will produce considerable action and reaction in the family or group.

PRACTICING SUMMARIZATION

1. *Develop a working group.*

2. *Assign roles* as helper, helpee, operator/observer, and second observer.

3. *Determine topic for role-play.* A very useful topic is your own career future and the decisions you need to make around it. Almost any decision you have to make which involves multiple dimensions, however, is appropriate.

4. *Task of the interviewer.* Begin the interview with an open question, use some paraphrases and other skills to bring out data, and then summarize what the role-played client says periodically, making sure to end the practice interview with a check-out.

5. *Watch time carefully and provide feedback.*

6. *Rotate roles.*

GROUP/FAMILY PRACTICE IN SUMMARIZATION

It is suggested that couple counseling be tried for this practice session. A family or group session could be attempted, but will involve a fairly long time for adequate problem development.

1. *Develop a working group.*

   a. Two members become the couple

   b. Helper

   c. Observer/recorder

2. *Determine topic for role-play.* Any type of couple conflict is appropriate for this practice session. The practice session will likely be more effective if the couple has a difference of opinion about an important decision—moving to a new job, having a child, making an important purchase, deciding where to spend vacation or how to spend money. Many couple problems occur in the process of making decisions.

3. *Planning.* The helper's task is to draw out the couple's conflict with as much information as possible. Ideally, the helper will want to know the facts of the situation as seen by each member of the couple, the feelings each has, and any reasons the couple can generate to explain the situation. The task is to draw out data and information, not to problem-solve.

   Particularly important for the helper is to summarize the conflicting points of view accurately so that each member of the couple feels heard. In addition, the helper should attempt to summarize the interaction of the couple and patterns that may be observed.

   During planning time, the role-played couple can generate a tentative "script" concerning their "difficulties." The observer can study the observer form and prepare any recording equipment.

4. *Watch time carefully and provide feedback.* The role-play should last approximately 10–15 minutes. Allow 15–20 minutes for feedback.

5. *Rotate roles as time permits.*

CLASSIFYING AND RATING SKILLS FOR QUALITY

As you view videotapes, listen to your own audiotapes, or watch a film, and practice classifying the leads of the helper as O?, C?, E, P, RF, and S. Use "Other" for skills that are other than those which you have practiced. To facilitate interview recall, write the main words of each helper response.

In addition, rate individual responses and the total interview on the following scale indicating your quality rating of the statement.

5	extremely helpful	Use of skills greatly adds to and enriches communication
4	very helpful	Use of skills adds to and enriches communication
3	helpful	Use of skills adds slightly to communication
2	less helpful	Use of skills detracts from communication (Frequent daily interpersonal interaction)
1	destructive	Use of skills disrupts and significantly hinders communication

Skill—Quality   KEY WORDS OF HELPER STATEMENTS

____ ____   1. _____

____ ____   2. _____

____ ____   3. _____

____ ____   4. _____

____ ____   5. _____

____ ____   6. _____

____ ____   7. _____

____ ____   8. _____

____ ____   9. _____

____ ____   10. _____

____ ____   11. _____

____ ____   12. _____

____ ____   13. _____

A DO-USE-TEACH CONTRACT

Do: I did use summarization during the practice sessions (when, where, and with what effect?):

_____

_____

_____

Use: You will find it helpful to practice summarization when you help others make important decisions. It may be helpful to make lists of positives and negatives of important decisions and use these written data as part of your summaries.

I plan to use this new skill outside this session in the following manner:

_____

_____

_____

Teach: You may want to think about how you could help train peer counselors or family members in listening skills and how the skill of summarization fits into your plans.

My plans to teach this important skill to someone else are as follows:

_____

_____

_____

Skill Classifications

3. S	11. O?	19. S
5. P and CO	13. P/O?	21. S—CO
7. P	15. P	23. E
9. S—O?	17. O?	25. S—CO

*The five stages of the interview
allow you and your client to
integrate what has been said
in a meaningful whole.*

*Can you complete a full session
using only listening skills?*

CHAPTER 7

INTEGRATION OF SKILLS:
STRUCTURING AN EFFECTIVE INTERVIEW

How do you put all the skills of this book together in a well-structured interview? This chapter provides specifics for organizing interviews that you can use both in sessions and in many interpersonal situations.

It is possible to conduct a complete and successful interview using only listening skills. The foundation skills of attending are basic to effective interviewing and the information in this book will often be enough to enable clients to solve problems and to change their behavior, thoughts, and feelings.

Why are the listening skills so important? We believe the first task of the helper is to listen to the helpee's story and understand her or his point of view, feelings, and concepts. If you listen carefully to others, you can help them understand their problems and discover new opportunities. Many times clients can make their own decisions and find new ways to take action if we listen effectively.

We suggest that if attending skills are not sufficient, then it may be time to move on to skills of interpersonal influence. A companion book *Basic Influencing Skills* discusses skills such as interpretation, self-disclosure, and feedback. Yet, even as you move to more action in the interview, the basic skills of attending and effective listening remain central.

The exercises and readings in this chapter will help you to:

1. Understand some problems and opportunities in the single skills approach to learning utilized in this book. You will be introduced to the "millipede effect."

2. Review the skills of this book as they are integrated in the *basic listening sequence.*

3. Define the structure of an effective interview.

4. Demonstrate that you can integrate the several listening skills in a full practice interview. You will also be encouraged to apply this framework in group and family sessions.

5. Use the five-stage structure of the interview in your daily life and in your own helping practice. Finally, we hope that you will consider teaching this structure to others as a way to improve their communication skills.

THE MILLIPEDE EFFECT

A millipede was walking happily along on a sunny day on its thousand legs. A fly flew by overhead and commented—"You certainly are clever, millipede. How on earth do you coordinate all those legs?"

The millipede responded, "Fly, I never thought of it before. I guess I just do it," and the fly buzzed off.

The millipede started to think, "The fly raises a good question. Now, do I alternate each leg down the line? Or do my left legs all go together and then the right? Just what do I do?"

The millipede collapsed and fell in the ditch. In the middle of all this thinking, the millipede's natural coordinated movement was disturbed.

Moral: *If you think too much about what you are doing, you may fall apart.*

The single microskills approach of this book has asked you to examine something you've done all your life without thinking about it. We naturally learn how to communicate and you may have found a temporary decrease in your skills when you focused on specific dimensions. That is a natural part of learning.

Perhaps you took piano lessons or ballet. There you must work on single skills. You learn the importance of pulling out scales or specific body movements and practicing them to perfection.

The same principles apply in tennis, basketball, golf, skiing, and other sports. The person with natural ability can improve at music, ballet, or sports if he or she is willing to take time out to practice single dimensions and truly master them. But, when single skills are first practiced, there is a temporary decrease in perform-ance and natural flow. Ultimately, natural abilities are improved by practice of important basic skills and the skills become integrated in the person.

And, this is so with *Basic Attending Skills.* When you think about and practice the skills for the first few times, expect some decrease in performance. But, if you continue your efforts with the skills, you will find a new level of expertise, often far beyond your original level. The skills will become integrated into your own natural style.

An important maxim for you to recall:

> *Skill practice may result in a temporary decrease in communication. However, if you work on the skills and learn them to near-perfection, they will become a natural part of you and you may find yourself a greatly improved communicator.*

THE BASIC LISTENING SEQUENCE: BASIC SKILL #7

You have practiced six specific skills with clients. All are based on a foundation of culturally appropriate attending behavior (eye contact, body language, vocal qualities, and verbal following). The next five skills are classified by their verbal structure: open invitation to talk, minimal encourage, paraphrase, reflection of feeling, and summarizations. In addition to these skills, the check-out has been stressed as an important addition to your listening skills to help clients respond more fully.

The basic listening sequence (BLS) is a way to integrate all the skills of this book in one useful package. The BLS was discovered while observing a manager at Digital Computer Corporation. An employee came up to the manager with a prob-lem on the production line. The manager engaged in good attending behavior and responded to the employee as follows:

> "Could you tell me about the problem on the production line?" *(open question)*

> "You say that the supply department hasn't given you enough comput-er chips to keep your group moving smoothly." *(paraphrase)*

"Uh-huh, tell me more about the defect." (*encourages* were used to facilitate exploration on some key words used by the employee)

"Sounds like the situation really makes you angry." (*reflection of feeling*)

The manager then *summarized* the employee's view of the problem and only then did the manager start to look toward problem solving. Notice that questions bring out the basic dimensions of the problem while the minimal encourage and paraphrase clarify what is occurring. Acknowledging or reflecting feeling brings out the emotional dimensions. Finally, the summary brings it all together so that the total situation can be reviewed accurately.

As you can see, the BLS is also an excellent way to summarize and integrate the concepts of this book. Not only are the concepts useful in management, but they are equally vital in the helping process. Counseling and psychotherapy are founded on the basic listening sequence.

The BLS also reminds us that we need to draw out the *facts* of the situation or problem and how the client *feels* about those facts. We can get this information through encouraging, questioning, paraphrasing and reflection of feeling. We also need to note how the client *organizes* these facts and feelings. It is here that the summarization is so helpful to both you and the client.

It may be helpful for you to think about the BLS and the specific listening goals of drawing out the facts, feelings, and organization of your client's concerns and issues. Interestingly, many times the sequence of questioning, encourage, paraphrasing, reflection of feeling, and summarization can be followed in systematic order. It is not recommended, however, that you follow the BLS order all the time, but knowledge of the BLS and the importance of facts, feelings, and organization should help you in a multitude of helping, counseling, and therapeutic situations.

THE FIVE-STAGE INTERVIEW STRUCTURE: BASIC SKILL #8

Interviews can be structured in many ways, but one effective framework consists of five stages. If you learn this one model, you can adapt it with many clients with widely varying issues and concerns. You will also find it useful in situations where you work with a person who is culturally different from you, but again it will have to be adapted to the unique person before you.

In outline form the structure appears as follows. Note that the basic listening sequence (BLS) is used again and again in this framework. As you examine the five-stage structure of the interview, keep in mind that it should serve as a check-list, a framework that you can shape to meet the needs of each individual with whom you work.

Definition of Stage	Goals in This Stage	Skills and Multicultural Issues at Stage
1. *Rapport and structuring.* "Hello. Let me tell you what we will do in this session."	Develop a working relationship with your client. Share with your client how the session will be structured and its general purpose. Some personal sharing about yourself may be needed with some clients culturally different from you or who may be hesitant to speak.	Culturally and individually appropriate attending behavior is the most important skill at this stage. You will want to generate an atmosphere of trust. With some clients that may take much longer than with others.
2. *Gathering information, defining the problem, and identifying assets.* "How can I help?" "What are some of your strengths?"	Obtain a clear summary of the client's story and issues. You will want to know the critical facts, feelings, and organization of the problem. Also, focus on positive strengths of the client.	The BLS will be especially helpful in discovering relevant data. Once the client's issues are fully understood, you are half-way there. With some clients, goal setting (Stage 3) may be completed first.
3. *Determining outcomes.* "What do you want to have happen?"	You don't know where you're going unless you have a goal. Interviews may be aimless unless you have a purpose for the client.	The BLS will be useful in drawing out client goals and how the client feels about and organizes these goals. A clear joint statement of goals can be especially useful when the client is different from you.

(continued)

Definition of Stage	Goals in This Stage	Skills and Multicultural Issues at Stage
4. *Exploring alternatives and generating solutions.* "What are the possibilities and what are you going to do about it?"	Having clarified the goal and the problem, you can turn to brainstorming solutions, making lists of possibilities, and prioritizing possible actions. This phase of the interview is usually the longest.	Again, the BLS will be critical. You will find that clients can often generate their own ideas if you use skillful questioning and encouraging. If the client misses obvious possibilities, you may at this point want to turn to influencing skills. Some clients, both culturally different and similar to you may want or demand your advice.
5. *Generalization and transfer of learning.* "Are you really going to do something about it?"	This is the phase of the interview which is most often forgotten. It is important to contract with your client to ensure that they act on learnings from the session.	Again, the BLS will be useful in working with your client to determine some future action. You may need to share the reasons for follow-up.

EXTENDING THE FIVE-STAGE INTERVIEW TO OTHER CONTEXTS

Although it was designed originally for full interviews, it is possible to use the five-stage structure of the interview in short contacts with helpees and even friends and family members who seek advice. When you are short of time and need to make contact with a client, recall the five stages as a checklist:

1. Do you spend some time in the contact on rapport and relationship? Time spent in developing personal relationships pays large dividends over time.

2. Do you draw out the facts, feelings, and organization of the client's problem? If you focus just on one dimension, you may lose valuable data.

3. Do you and the other person have a goal in mind or are you "just talking?" "If you don't know where you are going, you may end up somewhere else."

4. Do you allow clients to generate ideas on their own before you give them your suggestions or advice? If you listen to their concerns first, they may solve the issues on their own.

5. Do you suggest specific follow-up actions so that new and useful ideas are tested rather than forgotten?

When it comes to using the five-stage structure, you will have a large number of possibilities in your daily life outside of the interview.

USING THE FIVE STAGES WITH LESS VERBAL CLIENTS

In Chapter 3, suggestions are given for helping hesitant or less verbal clients in the interview. The importance of questions requiring shorter, concrete answers was mentioned. You will find those pages helpful in adapting the five-stage structure with less verbal clients.

At the rapport stage, for example, your own conversation should be concrete and clear with a minimum of abstract concepts. It can be helpful if you share a concrete experience of yours early on in the interview. If you stay at the concrete level, you will find that meanings between you and the client are more easily shared. Misunderstandings can arise when counselors talk in intellectualized, abstract language.

In defining the problem, search for specific examples. Be willing to listen to concrete, detailed stories from your clients. In that way, they can express themselves more clearly. In establishing goals, focus on items which are very specific and observable. An abstract goal would be "I want to get along better with my family," whereas a concrete goal would be "To get along with my family, I am going to start doing specific things with them (for example, playing games, helping around the house).

Brainstorming alternatives at the problem-solving stage can be a problem for the less verbal client. Help the client concretize ways to reach their aims by asking specific questions that can be answered relatively briefly. Rather than generate five alternative solutions quickly, focus on each one by itself and discuss it concretely in more detail before moving on.

For both verbal and less verbal clients, making very concrete plans for generalization and taking new learnings from the interview is important. Specify changes in behavior as concretely as possible indicating with whom, at what time, and in what place attempts to change will take place.

With children and adolescents, the suggestions above may be useful. As mentioned previously, younger children can talk more easily if they have toys, games, or art to use while they talk to you. Adolescents are often edgy and full of energy—it may be useful to have objects available for them to touch as they talk with you (but only if you have the ability to be patient with their "fiddling"). With many adolescents, it may be better to go out and play basketball, table tennis, or go for a walk rather than requiring them to sit quietly in your office.

STRUCTURING THE INTERVIEW WITH FAMILIES AND GROUPS

You will find that the five-stage structure of the interview is valuable when you plan a meeting or work with a group on problem-solving. It can even be helpful to list the five stages on newsprint or whiteboard to help keep group members on topic. It pays off to spend some time on structuring the meeting and on generating rapport and trust at the start of the meeting. If you do this, you'll find that a lot of time has been saved, as the group now knows the purpose of the session and each have had some important personal recognition. Often it helps to go around the room and have each member share something positive about him or herself or the family/group as you start the session.

When you gather information at the second stage, often group members will start problem-solving immediately. We suggest that they be gently asked to hold their ideas until the issues are defined fully. And, goal setting is equally important for if the group does not have a joint direction, the members will be heading "all over the place" with no common vision.

Once you have carefully brought out the problem and defined goals, exploring issues and new solutions becomes smoother and groups tend to work effectively if they have a common goal. Don't forget generalization and getting specifics for action as the meeting ends as follow-up is needed. All too often a productive meeting flounders because a specific action plan was not developed.

However, you will find that families and many groups do not follow the five stages as easily as do individuals. The diversity of interests and needs may lead to some people in the group being at the first rapport stage while someone else is ready to start brainstorming solutions.

Basic Attending Skills is not designed to make you an expert in group counseling. Nonetheless, you will find the foundation concepts helpful in dealing with both unstructured and structured groups.

Unstructured Groups

Group counseling usually occurs over several sessions with ten three-hour sessions being a common length. Those expert in group process note that unstructured groups (encounter, marathon, or "T-groups") often go through stages themselves that may or may not agree or be workable with the five stages discussed here. Many unstructured groups go through some variation of the following:

Forming. During the first stages of a group, particularly those that are unstructured or stranger groups, you will often find polite social interaction. However, the lack of leadership eventually leads to frustration. Attending skills and observations of group nonverbal behavior on the part of the leader may be useful here.

This group stage is parallel to the rapport/structuring phase of the interview as people are trying to know one another and find a structure for the group.

Storming. During the next stages of a group, particularly those that are unstructured or stranger groups, you will find considerable frustration as the group attempts to find itself and its direction. There is often a struggle for leadership and power. Your leadership skills of paraphrasing, reflection of feeling, and summarization are often useful here. The influencing skill of feedback may be particularly important—here the leader gives accurate feedback on what he or she observes in the group. Note the focus of leader comments is often on the *group as a whole* rather than on single individuals—"This *group* seems very angry right now."

In some ways storming is similar to the second stage of the five stages of the interview. The problem that the group wishes to work on may be defined, at least in preliminary form.

Norming. The group starts to settle down at this phase. Members share themselves more freely. Cohesiveness develops which makes problem definition and goal setting possible. Norming corresponds closely to stages 2 and 3 of the five-stage interview. Problems and group goals may be defined here.

The group members start working on their own interaction or on a joint problem. Norms and ways of interacting have been established and the leader can continue using the same skills as outlined earlier. If you have modeled effective listening and feedback, group members themselves may start using these same skills more effectively. *Your importance as a model of effective communication cannot be over stressed.*

Performing. This is the work stage of the group. Individuals may test out new behaviors. Disagreements may be worked out more constructively. Your focus on the group as a whole may pay important dividends here. Group members may start to look at themselves and how they relate to the total group process.

Again, your ability to listen and provide feedback is important. You may help the group and specific individuals examine how their behavior in the outside world is similar to their behavior in the here and now of the group.

Terminating/adjourning. As a group comes to the end, you will find that many of the old issues between members reappear and need to be worked through once again. The sense of loss when a group ends can be a problem for some members and old separation anxieties are brought out. The skills of summarization and reflection of feeling may be particularly important in helping a group work through this stage.

Unstructured groups can benefit from the concrete structuring of generalization offered within the five-stage interview. If each member can contract for a specific change or follow-up, the chances of long-term benefit from the group experience are greatly enhanced.

The listening skills emphasized in this book are important starting points for group and family work. As you develop more knowledge and expertise in the helping field, you'll find the information presented here on listening remains foundational.

Structured Groups

Structured groups also tend to meet with a defined period of time. The major distinction is that the topic is agreed to before the group starts. You may find yourself leading a group of high school or elementary students exploring their common concerns over family alcoholism or divorce. You may conduct a structured group in consciousness-raising for women, minorities, the developmentally challenged, or gays/lesbians. You may start a self-help group for cancer victims, families of Alzheimer's patients, or business people who have just lost their jobs.

You will find that the forming, storming, norming, performing, and adjourning concepts discussed above will also be a part of your work with structured groups, but usually, these stages are less pronounced as the group members often had varying goals when they joined. However, the surprise personal discoveries in a structured group often require you to use many of the same behaviors and leadership styles of the unstructured group process.

In structured groups, the five stages of the interview may be followed more closely, but you will find that entire sessions may focus on any one stage. For example, the entire first three-hour session is likely to focus on rapport building and learning how a particular group is to be structured. You will seldom, if ever, actually go through the entire five stages of the well-formed interview when working with a group.

Throughout this book, we have stressed that it is important to use the listening skills as group members talk in much the same way as you might use them when conducting individual sessions. We have also stressed that it is important to focus on the group as a whole. ("This group is anxious right now—everyone seems to want to avoid the pain and fear of the possibility of a cancer reoccurrence." "This group seems to be telling self-defeating stories—there are people who have learned how to grow beyond alcoholism.")

We have suggested in working with structured groups that you give one-third of your time to the group topic (cancer, divorce, eating problems, racism, sexism), one-third of the time to personal thoughts and feelings around the topic, and one-third of the time to group process—how the group itself deals with the topic.

You will find that you can use attending behavior and the skills of the basic listening sequence as your basic skill framework for much of your work with groups.

Family Sessions

Family counseling and therapy may be the most complex and difficult helping framework. Families move rapidly between forming, storming, norming, performing, and terminating, sometimes all in one interview. Families often will want to focus on an individual when they need to look at their family interaction. And when one individual needs attention, the family may turn to discussing some other topic.

Your listening and attending skills will serve as good foundations for family work, but you will want to study much further before you attempt to work in depth with family counseling. If you are trained in individual counseling, you may be tempted to focus on individuals. In group work, it is important to focus on the word "group." In family work, you will need to use the word "family" again and again to help the individuals focus on their interactions rather than on a single family member.

In your role-plays and practice sessions, the five stages of the interview are workable frameworks for practice in family counseling:

1. *Rapport/structuring.* It is wise to spend time in a family session developing some sort of individual rapport with each member. At the same time you want to *join* the family as a temporary member and this means seeing yourself as both a family member *and* as an observer.

2. *Problem definition.* Many families come to counseling with an "identified patient," perhaps the family alcoholic, the bulimic, or the acting-out child or adolescent. Many family therapists ask each member of the family to define the problem. They listen carefully and reflect back to each person what they have just said. Later the counselor often summarizes the varying family perspectives and reframes or reinterprets the individual issues as a

family problem. *The focus moves from the individual to the family interaction itself.*

The problem definition phase is vital in family work, perhaps even more so than in individual counseling. You will be tempted to focus on single individuals and their problems. Family therapy stresses the importance of seeing any individual issue always in the context of family.

3. *Establishing goals.* A process very similar to the above occurs in setting up family goals. Each person has her or his say and then the counselor helps the family establish joint family goals for more effective interaction. For example, instead of stopping an adolescent from acting-out, the goal of the family turns to becoming a family that works together more effectively.

4. *Exploring alternatives.* There are many theories and practices in family work that you will want to study and master. As you begin, your ability to listen will remain vital. If you listen effectively and focus on the family as a whole, often the family will begin to generate its own solutions.

Balancing your listening between family, individuals, and the topic (the family problem) will be helpful both as you begin and as you master family therapy. The counselor needs to balance focus on the agreed-on family topic (for example, how can this family work together more effectively and not be so focused on acting-out, bulimia, alcoholism, etc.), individual members' thoughts and feelings, and specific instances of family group interaction here and now in the session with the counselor which relate either to individual reactions or the agreed-upon topic.

5. *Generalization.* Families seem to benefit from concrete homework assignments so that they can take what they have learned in the group/family situation and apply it at home.

In summary, structured and unstructured groups and family sessions are indeed different from individual counseling and therapy. Yet, the skills you learn in individual work can be applied rather directly to groups and families. Again, it is important that you engage in further study and practice in this complex area. The material here is designed as a brief introduction to some of the key concepts of work with more than one individual.

PRACTICE AND FOLLOW-UP WITH SKILL INTEGRATION

The task of this session is to demonstrate that you can conduct a full practice helping session using only attending and listening skills.

1. *Develop a working group.* To practice integration of skills, it will take more time. While groups of four are most desirable, it may be necessary to work in triads or pairs.

2. *Assign roles* as helper, helpee, operator/observer, and second observer.

3. *Determine topic for role-play.* The five-stages of the interview are particularly effective in helping a client make a decision. Some useful decision topics include career choice, making a major purchase, deciding how to handle a specific interpersonal conflict, or your future as a professional helper.

   The following specific guidelines may be helpful for the role-played counselor:

   a. Rapport/structure. Spend necessary time tuning yourself in with the client in your own way and inform him or her of the purpose of the interview.

   b. Defining the problem. Use the BLS to draw out the client's issue. Be sure to spend some time defining client strengths. Remember that the concrete question, "Could you give me a specific example?" used in varying form will be useful in all stages of the interview to expand and clarify what is happening.

   c. Determining outcomes. Again, the BLS can be helpful in drawing out what the client sees as a goal or ideal outcome.

   d. Exploring alternatives and generating solutions. Begin this section by summarizing the problem and the outcomes as desires. Ask the open question, "Could you tell me what ideas/possibilities for resolution come to your mind?" You will find that the organization of the problem offered by the BLS and the five-stage structure often helps many clients find new and workable problem solutions here.

 e. Generalization. Through attending skills and questioning, help your client define something specific he or she might do during the coming week to implement the ideas generated.

4. *Provide as much time as needed and provide feedback.*

5. *Rotate roles.*

GROUP/FAMILY PRACTICE IN STRUCTURING THE INTERVIEW

It is suggested that couple counseling be tried for this practice session. A group or family session could be attempted, but will involve a fairly long time for adequate discussion.

1. *Develop a working group.*

  a. Two members become the couple

  b. Helper

  c. Observer/recorder

2. *Determine topic for role-play.* Similar topics as used for summarization are suggested. Any type of couple conflict is appropriate for this practice session. The practice session will likely be more effective if the couple has a difference of opinion about an important decision—moving to a new job, having a child, making an important purchase, where to spend vacation, or how to spend money. Many couple problems occur in the process of making decisions.

3. *Planning.* The helper's task is to draw out the couple's conflict with as much information as possible. Ideally, the helper will want to know the facts of the situation as seen by each member of the couple, the feelings each has, and any reasons the couple can generate to explain what is occurring. The task is to draw out data and information, not to problem-solve.

Particularly important for the helper is to summarize the conflicting points of view accurately so that each member of the couple feels heard. In addition, the helper should attempt to summarize the interaction of the couple and patterns that may be observed.

Use the same suggestions for structuring the interview as were summarized above for the individual session. But adapt the structure to meet the needs of the couple. You will find that the summarization skill is particularly important in couple, family, and group interviews.

During planning time, the role-played couple can generate a tentative "script" concerning their "difficulties." The observer can study the observer form and prepare any recording equipment.

4. *Watch time carefully and provide feedback.* The role-play should last approximately 10–15 minutes. Allow 15–20 minutes for feedback.

5. *Rotate roles as time permits.*

SKILL INTEGRATION FEEDBACK SHEET

Use the following form to classify the skills of the helper. Make a note on the form when a new stage of the interview begins. Classify the leads of the helper as O?,C?,E,P,RF, and S. Use "Other" for skills that are other than those which you have practiced. Write the main words of each helper response. In addition, rate individual responses and the total interview on the following five-point scale indicating your quality rating of the statement.

5	maximally facilitative	Use of skills greatly adds to and enriches communication
4	facilitative	Use of skills adds to and enriches communication
3	minimally facilitative	Use of skills adds slightly to communication
2	non-facilitative	Use of skills detracts from communication (Frequent daily interpersonal interaction)
1	destructive	Use of skills disrupts and significantly hinders communication

Skill—Quality   *KEY WORDS OF HELPER STATEMENTS*

____ ____   1. _____

____ ____   2. _____

____ ____   3. _____

____ ____   4. _____

____ ____   5. _____

____ ____   6. _____

____ ____   7. _____

____ ____   8. _____

____ ____   9. _____

____ ____ 10. _____

____ ____ 11. _____

____ ____ 12. _____

Continue on a separate sheet of paper using the same format.

Repeated below are suggestions for the five stages of the interview. Comment on the success of the interview in achieving the objectives of each stage.

1. Rapport/structure. Spend necessary time tuning yourself in with the client in your own way and inform him or her of the purpose of the interview. How well was this objective achieved?

_____

_____

2. Defining the problem. Use the BLS to draw out the client's issue. Be sure to spend some time defining client strengths. Remember that the concrete question, "Could you give me a specific example?" used in varying form will be useful in all stages of the interview to expand and clarify what is happening. How well was this objective achieved?

_____

_____

3. Determining outcomes. Again, the BLS can be helpful in drawing out what the client sees as a goal or ideal outcome. How well was this objective achieved?

_____

_____

4. Exploring alternatives and generating solutions. Begin this section by summarizing the problem and the outcomes as desires. Ask the open question, "Could you tell me what ideas/possibilities for resolution come to your mind?" You will find that the organization of the problem offered by the BLS and the five-stage structure often helps many clients find new and workable problem solutions here. How well was this objective achieved?

_____

_____

_____

5. Generalization. Through attending skills and questioning, help your client define something specific he or she might do during the coming week to implement the ideas generated. How well was this objective achieved?

_____

_____

_____

DO-USE-TEACH CONTRACT

Your primary emphasis as you complete this book needs to focus on the *use* dimension of the contract. How can you continue to use the skills you have acquired? How can you incorporate them into your daily life and in practical work in interviewing practice?

However, incorporating and truly making the skills of this workshop series part of you will take some time. It will require you to practice the skills deliberately. For these purposes the rating and count sheets used in this workshop can be most helpful. Copy them and use them as you examine your own interviewing style.

Whenever you have the opportunity—perhaps even tonight at home with your spouse or friend—audiotape or videotape a session. Analyze the interaction for yourself and teach the other person how to analyze the session as well. Take a look at yourself at home, at work, and watch your helping style emerge.

What we are suggesting here is that you become your own teacher, your own advocate. Select the behaviors and skills you like, that seem to work for you. Change them, adapt them to make them your own. Ultimately, you must act alone; perhaps by starting a simple process of self-observation you can maintain and continue your growth as a helper and in this way you can come into closer touch with others.

Would you be willing to share one thing that you see as most important for you to follow up from this book?

_____

_____

_____

How do you see yourself using the ideas of this book in the future? (Now, three months, one year?)

_____

_____

_____

*Teaching helping skills to others is
one effective client treatment strategy.
Think—"Training as Treatment."*

*This chapter shows you how to
train individuals, families, small groups,
and perhaps even community volunteers
in these basic skills
of personal communication and interviewing.*

CHAPTER 8

TEACHING HELPING SKILLS TO OTHERS

This chapter is for the instructor and for those students who want to teach communication skills to others. Microcounseling is a scaled-down interviewing session in which a beginning counselor talks with a volunteer client about real problems. The interview occurs in a setting that provides interviewing practice with maximum opportunity for immediate feedback and trainee growth. The compressed nature of the situation allows a focus on specific dimensions of interviewing skills and does not demand that the trainee respond immediately as a fully professional counselor.

The central purpose of this book (and accompanying videos) is to provide helpers with a basic orientation to the skills approach to helping. By the end of each session, the beginning helper should have a specific understanding of a single skill and the ability to demonstrate that skill and classify specific behavior in an interview.

The extended objectives are defined in the "Do-Use-Teach Contracts." The effort here does not end with teaching of skills in a classroom or workshop setting. We hope that people actually do use them and seriously consider teaching them to others—their clients, volunteer peer and entry-level helpers, and even professional colleagues. Our experience reveals that even many doctoral level professionals have more work to do on their basic skills.

Thus the objectives of the video and written materials are double—to teach specific skills and to provide methods by which those who have learned the skills can teach them to others.

TEACHING AS TREATMENT

Basic Attending Skills is a foundation course in communication skills. We have found that teaching each of these skills to both outpatient and inpatient populations is a very effective adjunct to traditional counseling and therapy. Attending behavior and questioning skills are particularly helpful to clinically depressed clients. It is difficult to be depressed and focused on oneself when one is attending to someone else.

When you work with clients, many of them will have patterns of poor attending behavior. They may have poor eye contact or be unable to stay on the topic. Teaching the skills of attending can make a real difference in their daily lives. To teach skills such as attending behavior or questioning, recall the following framework:

1. Tell your client or patient what you are going to do and why. You are going to teach them a basic skill of communication that can make a real difference in how they relate to others. Many of your clients have relationship problems. One route toward better social and family relationships is effective listening.

2. Define the skill clearly to them. Distressed clients may not be able to learn all four dimensions of attending behavior. If so, teach only one concept at a time.

3. Model the skill for them. Demonstrate poor listening and then demonstrate effective listening.

4. Have the client practice the skill with you in a role-play. The client may profit from demonstrating poor skills first and then more effective skills.

5. Assign homework so that clients can practice the skills in their home settings.

A wide number of populations have benefited from learning communication skills. People as varied as parents and elementary children, convicts and priests, men who batter their families and women's consciousness-raising groups have all profited from learning these skills. Such skill training does not solve serious underlying problems, but does provide specific alternatives that can be part of problem solution.

Many of the clients who come to the counselor or therapist lack effective listening skills. You will find many individual clients, families, and groups that can learn about themselves and others through training in the *Basic Attending Skills*.

As a trainer, we urge you to consider helping your trainees learn how to teach skills either on a one-on-one basis or in small groups.

KEY ASPECTS OF THE TEACHING PROCESS

For what populations are the skill units designed? We have tried to write materials, design video mini-lectures, and present models so that the training sessions and workshops may be suitable for a variety of people. Beginning helpers, teachers, parents, peer counselors, psychiatric aides, nurses, minority advocates, and high school students represent only a sampling of the wide variety of populations with whom these concepts have proven successful.

Although the concepts can be used with a wide variety of trainee populations and cultural groups, it must be recognized that the examples and video models tend to represent primarily middle-class concepts and values. These materials, however, have been used successfully with a variety of trainees.

This book has been translated into over a dozen languages in many cultures and situations. Among the many uses are training for:

- UNESCO AIDS counselors in Africa

- Aboriginal social workers in Australia and Inuit trainees in Canada

- Top management officials working with Erikksen Telephone in Sweden

- County extension workers

- Nurses and physicians (data indicate that better patient results occur with microskill trained hospital staff)

- Peer counselors in multiple settings including crisis counselors, senior citizen groups, library volunteers—literally, an endless array of training settings

Two more specific examples include: Norma Gluckstern has used the materials in training alcoholism counselors and has had success in teaching institutionalized convicts. Mary Bradford Ivey has adapted the concepts for teaching sixth grade children basic listening skills in a peer tutoring program. You may wish to adapt these materials and supplement them with specific examples more relevant to the groups with whom you work.

With more advanced groups such as clinical psychology trainees, medical students, counselor educators, these same materials have been used successfully.

The vocabulary of the leader changes and adaptations of some exercises may be necessary. However, when working with such groups, emphasis is on the *teaching role* of the professional. Advanced students appear to enjoy and benefit most from a workshop where they both learn skills for themselves and think about teaching helping skills to others. The professional helper is increasingly called upon to run workshops and train a wide variety of volunteer and lay populations.

How large a group can be taught using these materials? These workshops were planned for use with groups of approximately 20 people. However, the materials have been used with as few as one or two or with groups of up to 200 or more with appropriate adaptations.

A workshop could be managed with one leader and one video machine. The specificity of exercises and peer feedback gives virtually every participant a chance for significant experiential participation. Ideally, however, one leader for each 10–12 people is better. It is possible for the senior leader to train assistant leaders from the trainee population before the formal workshop.

What equipment is necessary? Ideal equipment would be a closed circuit video unit for every four people. This would ensure that everyone gets on video several times. One unit for ten or twelve should permit each member to be on video once. Beyond that, it is best to recognize that everyone can't be on video and accept the fact that demonstrations are the only possibility with a small number actually seeing themselves. Thus a workshop could be run with only one T.V. unit. More and more educational institutions and businesses have video labs where people can sign up for practice sessions, thus allowing for more flexible scheduling.

Training workshops and class designs here can be run with no video equipment at all. Then, live demonstrations can be used to present the skills in action. And, of course, audio recorders provide a most useful supplement if video is not available.

In addition, newsprint, masking tape, and felt markers are most useful and provide visual variety and interest. You may wish to make PowerPoint slides or overheads to supplement the session. If each trainee has a copy of *Basic Attending Skills,* this will make the workshop flow more easily and the feedback sheets are critical for skills development.

The importance of practice. While we recommend video as the most effective medium, several researchers have found that verbal skills can be learned equally effectively using audiotape. We ourselves have found that simply telling people clearly and directly what is to be learned is often effective. Nonetheless, the multimedia approach of microcounseling with video appears to be the most enjoyable and successful method for involving people over a period of time.

Whether these videos and materials are used in one-to-one counselor training or in workshop format, it is highly desirable that all participants have allotted time wherein they can practice videotaping counseling sessions outside of the immediate training situation. We have found that peer supervision is effective in supplementing formal microcounseling training.

THE BASIC MICROSKILL TRAINING FORMAT

Each workshop is structured with the following steps:

1. *Warm-up/orientation.* The introductory pages of the chapter may be read. An elementary exercise may be used to warm up individuals for the workshop or training they are about to receive.

2. *Reading.* Each chapter contains a short discussion of the basic skill. We suggest that the participants reread these brief manuals silently before viewing the video or seeing a live demonstration.

3. *Viewing of video model or live demonstration.* Each skill is demonstrated so that participants can see the skill in action. If the video is not available, it is suggested that you as trainer do a live demonstration. You may want to make videos of yourself and different students for demonstration purposes.

4. *Practice.* Specific suggestions for practicing each skill are included in each chapter. Go over these practice instructions with the trainees carefully in the early sessions of training. Then, when they have more experience, the groups will basically "run themselves." Note skill feedback sheets for each chapter.

5. *Do-Use-Teach.* Some workshop leaders fail to use this portion of microtraining which helps ensure behavioral leaning and retention.

6. *Evaluation.* An evaluation form to obtain feedback about the chapter and your work as a leader are at the end of this chapter.

Chapter 7, *Integration of Skills,* follows a somewhat more complex pattern and will be reviewed in more detail later.

Teaching Group and Family Skills. Each chapter has a section on adapting attending and listening skills for group and family practice. With beginning helpers, it is usually wise to skip this material, perhaps mentioning it briefly. But, as your trainees gain experience, they will want to attempt some of the group and family exercises.

Is it necessary to follow the precise ordering and procedures of these work-shops? We firmly believe that each leader/trainer must adapt the suggested exercises to fit unique personality styles and situations. Those experienced in workshop development will want to change exercises and the order of activities almost immediately. Those just starting this type of workshop may want to follow the guidelines fairly precisely the first few times, but will later move to personal adaptations.

Our experience is that the general type of format presented here is usually quite successful with groups. It provides a reasonable balance of cognitive input with practice and time for people to practice and discuss issues. Nonetheless, each leader must be prepared to adapt materials as the workshop progresses. No one way is right. With experience, the "sense of the group" can be developed and exercises arranged to fit these needs as they appear.

How much time does it take to cover the materials in this book? With a tight schedule, it is possible to complete the six basic workshops in six two to three-hour sessions. It is preferable, of course, to have more time. The shorter framework is effective when you have able, hard-working people who want to learn a maximum of information in a minimum of time. The problem with this intensive approach is that time for practice sessions is minimized and serious negotiation on the "do-use-teach" contracts becomes almost impossible.

Thus 20–40 hours is an appropriate time to cover the information provided here in depth while allowing for real mastery of the skills. Extra training time should be given primarily to providing individuals with a substantial amount of practice in the skills.

Originally we had suggested specific lengths of time for each exercise. We found through experience that some exercises can take ten minutes with one group and two hours with another. As such, the leader will have to select exercises and adapt them to fit the special needs and interests of each group.

Ethical questions. The workshop trainer should remember that we are working with people and usual standards for ethical conduct for training in counseling and group procedures hold. You may wish to go over some of the key ethical issues presented earlier in this book. Perhaps most important is the trainer being available to provide support and follow-up for any individuals who need or desire further counseling assistance.

At this point, it seems appropriate to turn to specific suggestions for teaching each chapter of the book.

TEACHING SUGGESTIONS FOR CHAPTER 2: ATTENDING BEHAVIOR

As this is the first training session, it is suggested that time first be spent in acquainting the group with one another. You will want to define the microtraining process as outlined in Chapter 1 so that your trainees are aware of the process.

The microtraining process may be summarized as follows:

1. *Warm-up/orientation.* Discuss the objectives of the first training session. Participants may want to share with the group or one another personal positive and negative experiences associated with listening and non-listening. A useful and humorous exercise is the demonstration "What Listening Is Not?" as presented in the chapter. Summarize the group's or individual's observation.

2. *Reading.* Participants read or reread Basic Skill #1 on Attending Behavior and discuss its implications. Rapid readers may continue on to reread other parts of the chapter again. You may want to conduct a lecture/discussion to supplement the reading.

3. *Viewing of video or live model.* Show video model of the skill. Or, if unavailable, demonstrate the skill via live modeling.

4. *Practice.* Group instructions for practice are presented in detail in each chapter. If working with one individual, follow the same framework, but you

will serve as the client and have to provide feedback yourself. With groups, stress the importance of written feedback using the feedback sheet. If on your own, still complete the written feedback for the other person.

5. *Do-Use-Teach.* Read through the ideas with your trainees, in pairs or groups of four, have each person develop a written contract to take the ideas of the workshop out beyond the training session.

6. *Evaluation.* Ask the participants to complete the evaluation form and turn them in to you. Permission to Xerox the evaluation form is granted.

TEACHING SUGGESTIONS FOR CHAPTERS 3–6

The format for each of these chapters remains the same as in Chapter 2. We have structured this fourth edition of *Basic Attending Skills* to simplify and clarify instructions. You will want to change format from time to time. Yet it is our experience over literally hundreds of workshops, classes, and training experiences that the simple framework is always the best over the long run.

The basic framework is:

1. Warm-up/orientation

2. Reading the skill manual in the training session itself (it seems to develop better retention and learning than just prereading)

3. Viewing of video model (or live demonstration)

4. Practice (have your students work toward mastery because going through the skills is not enough. And in the practice can the student make an impact on the client's conversation?)

5. Do-use-teach (the hardest part of the framework to maintain consistent use—develop a variety of ways to ensure transfer of training)

6. Evaluation. This framework works, produces results, seems to be interesting to students, is clear enough that students are able to use it themselves to teach others, provides a general model for teaching other skills and subject matter areas, and yet seems flexible enough to provide room for change.

Please recall that working with a single client or family with these skills can be helpful. This is especially true of attending behavior and questioning skills. If a person has the ability to listen to another person, this is an important start toward mental health and more effective personal relationships.

TEACHING SUGGESTIONS FOR CHAPTER 7

Given the structure of this chapter, it is likely that it will take you more than one session to complete the tasks suggested. The following order of exercises is suggested:

1. Divide into groups and provide time for get-acquainted or warm-up exercises as needed.

2. Read the Basic Skill summaries on the basic listening sequence and the five stages of the interview.

3. View the video model. Discuss the video and the interview structure. If you did not make a video record, discuss each phase of the session with your group and be sure to give special attention to nonverbal behavior.

4. The first time through, we have found it wise to have trainees work in pairs. Rather than go through an entire interview without stopping, we discuss each stage of the interview and have them practice that one phase. We stop after each stage for feedback. In this way, the stages are separated clearly and the objectives for each stage are achieved more easily. We have found in the early phases that trainees may move randomly from stage to stage unless the session is highly structured.

5. With the practice above as a background, we can then conduct a regular practice session with observers and feedback sheets.

6. Develop "Do-Use-Teach" contracts as indicated.

7. Evaluate the session(s).

The practice session for integration of skills and the five steps of the interview generally take longer than single skill practice. It is suggested that trainees repeat the process until they have mastered it to a high level. It is our belief that people should not move on to the influencing skills until they have thoroughly mastered the basic skills of the interview.

TEACHING HOW TO TEACH SKILLS

The Do-Use-Teach contract may be used as is. However, we prefer at this point to require our trainees to teach one another the skills of microtraining. We have found that this may be done even in a workshop setting using the following sequence:

1. Divide your group, regardless of size, into groups of four.

2. Two people in each group will select a skill that they would like to teach the other pair. The other two people select a skill they would like to teach to the first pair.

3. Planning time of about 30 minutes is allotted. During this time, the pairs plan a workshop consisting of: a) a warm-up exercise; b) reading this book coupled with some didactic presentation; c) live modeling of the skill; and d) supervised practice using feedback sheets.

4. The pair presents its skill workshop to the other pair.

5. The roles reverse.

We have found teaching experience that reassures beginners that they actually can teach others counseling and communication skills can be completed successfully in about two hours. Trainees are then prepared to go out and teach these skills beyond the workshops to parents, teachers, children, professionals, and a wide array of groups.

USING TRANSCRIPTS TO ENSURE TRAINEE MASTERY

An all-too-common tendency in counseling training is for the trainer to present information and assume that competency in the concept will develop. This is not necessarily so.

We require students to bring in transcripts or audiotapes weekly. In these transcripts or tapes they demonstrate that they can use the skill in question for positive client benefit. Such presentations take time to examine and provide feedback, yet their benefit for trainee growth cannot be denied.

At the conclusion of our course of training, we like to have our students present an interview transcript in which they demonstrate that they can conduct an interview using primarily, if not all, attending skills. We look to have students who are able to classify their skill usage. We also like students to discuss some of the theoretical and practical implications of their demonstrated helping practices. Each student should also make a critique of the session pointing out strengths and areas for improvement. The value of a typescript analysis cannot be over-emphasized.

FEEDBACK FORM ON ATTENDING AND LISTENING SKILLS

Name _____ Skill area evaluated _____
        (optional)

1. One thing in my behavior that I want to continue and see as a strength is:

2. One thing in my behavior that I plan to change or work to improve as a result of this session is:

3. The most helpful incident in this training was:

4. If I were conducting this training, one thing I would add would be:

5. As follow-up, I am going to *use* the ideas from this workshop in this specific plan of action:

6. As follow-up, I am going to *teach* the ideas from this workshop to this specific group or person in this specific fashion:

7. Use reverse side of sheet for additional comments and/or suggestions.